# DISCOVER THE BIBLE

AN ILLUSTRATED ADVENTURE FOR KIDS

# DISCOVER THE BIBLE

**AN ILLUSTRATED ADVENTURE FOR KIDS**

TRACY M. SUMNER

SHILOH kidz
An Imprint of Barbour Publishing, Inc.

© 2011 by Barbour Publishing, Inc.

Previously published under the title *Kids' Bible Handbook*.

ISBN 978-1-64352-220-3

All rights reserved. No part of this publication may be reproduced or transmitted for commercial purposes, except for brief quotations in printed reviews, without written permission of the publisher.

Churches and other noncommercial interests may reproduce portions of this book without the express written permission of Barbour Publishing, provided that the text does not exceed 500 words and that the text is not material quoted from another publisher. When reproducing text from this book, include the following credit line: "From *Discover the Bible*, published by Barbour Publishing, Inc. Used by permission."

Unless otherwise indicated, all scripture quotations are taken from the *Holy Bible*. New Living Translation copyright© 1996, 2004 by Tyndale House Foundation. Used by permission of Tyndale House Publishers, Inc. Carol Stream, Illinois 60188. All rights reserved.

Scripture quotations marked NKJV are taken from the New King James Version®. Copyright © 1982 by Thomas Nelson, Inc. Used by permission. All rights reserved.

Scripture quotations marked NIV are taken from the HOLY BIBLE, NEW INTERNATIONAL VERSION®. NIV®. Copyright © 1973, 1978, 1984 by Biblica, Inc.™ Used by permission. All rights reserved worldwide.

Scripture quotations marked NCV are taken from the New Century Version of the Bible, copyright © 2005 by Thomas Nelson, Inc. Used by permission. All rights reserved.

Scripture quotations marked MSG are from THE MESSAGE. Copyright © by Eugene H. Peterson 1993, 1994, 1995, 1996, 2000, 2001, 2002. Used by permission of NavPress Publishing Group.

Interior design and layout by ThinkPen Design.

Editorial cover credit, left photo: shutterstock.com

Published by Shiloh Kidz, an imprint of Barbour Publishing, Inc., 1810 Barbour Drive, Uhrichsville, Ohio 44683, www.shilohkidz.com

*Our mission is to inspire the world with the life-changing message of the Bible.*

Printed in China.

06682 1119 HA

# WHAT'S IN THIS BOOK

**Before You Get Started** .................................................................................. 7

**CHAPTER 1. How Did We Get This Book Anyway?**
The Work God Did—and the People He Used—to Give Us the Bible ................. 9

**CHAPTER 2. In the Beginning...and Beyond:**
How It All Started (Genesis through Deuteronomy) .................................... 19

**CHAPTER 3. His Story...and Their Story:**
The History of God's People (Joshua through Esther) .................................. 37

**CHAPTER 4. Words to Live By:**
God's Written Wisdom (Job through Song of Solomon) ................................ 55

**CHAPTER 5. God's Messengers:**
Major and Minor Prophets (Isaiah through Malachi) ................................... 67

**CHAPTER 6. The Bible's Main Man:**
The Story of Jesus (Matthew through John) ............................................... 83

**CHAPTER 7. How the Church Got Its Start**
(Acts of the Apostles) ............................................................................ 93

**CHAPTER 8. Letters That Became Books of the Bible:**
Epistles from Paul, Peter, and the Rest (Romans through Jude) .................. 103

**CHAPTER 9. What's Ahead:**
John's Vision of the Last Days (Revelation) ............................................. 123

**CHAPTER 10. Why You Should Read the Bible for Yourself...and How to Do It!** ........ 135

**APPENDIX A: Through the Bible in a Year: A 365-Day Bible-Reading Schedule** ....... 145

**APPENDIX B: Timeline of Important Biblical Events** ........................................ 156

**APPENDIX C: Important Dates (and Facts) in Bible Writing, Translation, and Publishing** .... 158

**Art Credits** ............................................................................................. 160

# BEFORE YOU GET STARTED

**Chances are, you've** got at least one copy somewhere in your home. Maybe more than one copy. And maybe more than one version.

What are we talking about?

The bestselling book of all time.

The Bible!

It only makes sense that the Bible, also called "God's Word" or "the Word of God," is the world's all-time bestseller. After all, it's been around for almost 2,000 years (actually, the books of the Old Testament have been around for a lot longer than that) and has been translated into hundreds of languages.

The Bible is easy to find in most parts of the world. In America, we have dozens of translations and styles available in just about any bookstore. There are study Bibles, children's Bibles, pocket-size Bibles, hardcover and softcover Bibles, and Bibles that include easy-to-follow reading plans for people who want to read through the entire Bible in a year.

Did you know that the word *Bible* actually means "book"? In reality, the Bible isn't just one book. It's a collection of 66 books (39 in the Old Testament and 27 in the New Testament), written by about 40 different writers over a period of several centuries. The oldest books of the Bible (including Job and the first five books of the Old Testament) were written 3,000 to 3,100 years ago; and the youngest book (Revelation, written by the apostle John) was written around 2,000 years ago.

We'll get into more detail about the Bible's writers and when they did their writing later on, but first let's focus on what the Bible means to us.

If someone were to ask you what the Bible is (other than a book that's been around for a really long time), how would you answer? Would you say that the Bible is a collection of stories about God's people going back thousands of years? Would you say it's God's book of promises for people who put their faith in

Him? Would you say it's a book of God's commands for people who want to please Him in the way they live, talk, and think?

Well, none of those answers would be wrong. In fact, they're all 100 percent correct. But there's a lot more to the Bible than that. You see, the Bible is more than a collection of stories about a bunch of people who died a long time ago, and it's more than a book of God's promises and commands. The Bible is the account of how God has communicated with the most prized part of His creation—His people!—from the beginning of time until the beginning of the Christian church. And it's also about how God communicates with you and me today.

With so many Bibles in the world, it's easy sometimes to start taking God's Word for granted. That's partly why I've written *this* book. I want to help you come to a greater appreciation for the Bible, and I want to give you some of the basics that will help you understand where it came from, how it became the book it is today, and how you can better read the Bible and understand what it is all about.

This book will give you a brief look at all 66 books of the Bible, including information about the people who wrote the books, the men and women they were written to, what the books mean, and how the message of the Bible applies to your life today.

Each of the 10 chapters in this book includes a story about how the Bible came to be, as well as some fun and interesting features about the Bible and what you'll find in it.

Here are some of the fun features you'll find in this book:

**Power Words:** Important verses you can memorize from different books of the Bible.

**Who, What, Where?** Important people, things, and places mentioned in the Bible, as well as the people and events God used to give us the Bible.

**Fun Bible Trivia:** Some not-so-well-known facts about people and events you can find in the Bible.

**What's in It for Me?** How you can apply what you read in the Bible to your own life.

**Did You Know. . . ?** Fun facts about the Bible itself and how it came to be the book it is today.

This book won't teach you everything there is to know about the Bible. To do that, it would have to be many times longer than it is. What it will do, though, is give you a good place to start as you read, study, and learn what the Bible has to say and what it means to you.

When you're finished reading this book, you'll have a pretty good idea of how wonderful and amazing the Bible really is. And you'll probably think to yourself, *Wow! The Bible is a really cool book!*

# CHAPTER 1

## How Did We Get This Book Anyway?

The Work God Did—and the People He Used—to Give Us the Bible

**Take a look** at your own copy of the Bible. If you don't have it nearby, take a minute to go get it. Then just look at it for a moment. You've probably read at least some of the Bible, and you might even have a pretty good idea about what it says. But have you ever stopped to think about what it took to give you an opportunity to have your very own copy?

A lot of Christians, even some who know the Bible very well, don't really understand how we got the 66 books that make up the Bible. That's what this chapter is all about. It gives you a quick look at how God used different people from all sorts of backgrounds to record His words, to gather them all together to make up one book, and to help make the Bible available in the language that you speak, write, and read.

So read on! You're about to discover the amazing story of how God's Word became the book we know as the Bible.

## Writing Down God's Words

**The first thing** you should know about the Bible—if you don't already—is that God didn't just give someone a completed manuscript and send him off to a printing press. Actually, the story of how we got the Bible is a lot more interesting than that.

You probably know—even if you haven't given it a lot of thought—that someone had to write down the words that are in your Bible. Actually, the books of the Bible were written by about 40 men (and possibly a few women). These writers came from a lot of different backgrounds and professions. For example, Moses was a shepherd, Amos was a fig farmer, Matthew was a tax collector, and Peter and John were fishermen.

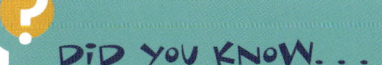

**DID YOU KNOW. . . ?**

The apostle Paul writes, "All Scripture is inspired by God" (2 Timothy 3:16). The idea behind the word *inspiration* is that God "breathed out" or "spoke" the words that are in the Bible. In other words, the words you read in the Bible are the words of God Himself!

Yet all these people, from different backgrounds, writing over a span of about 1,500 years, together produced a unified book that never disagrees with itself, never moves from its main message, and always presents God's perfect plan for the salvation of humanity.

How did such a group of writers—most of whom never met one another—pull that off? The answer to that question is in the word *inspiration*. One of the Bible's main writers, the apostle Paul, writes, "All Scripture is *given* by *inspiration of* God" (2 Timothy 3:16, italics added). What Paul means is that God, through His Holy Spirit, spoke through the Bible's writers and gave them His very own words to record. In other words, the people who wrote the books of the Bible were tools that God miraculously used to give us His written Word.

This means that, even though the Bible was written by dozens of people from different backgrounds and points of view, it has one ultimate author: God Himself. That's why you can count on the Bible as your final source for everything you need to know about how to live a life that pleases God.

### POWER WORDS
*No prophecy in Scripture ever came from the prophet's own understanding, or from human initiative. No, those prophets were moved by the Holy Spirit, and they spoke from God.*
2 Peter 1:20–21

## Why *These* Books?

**All 39 of** the books in the Old Testament had been written by about 400 BC (*before* the birth of Christ), and all 27 of the New Testament books were finished by the end of the first century AD (*after* the birth of Christ).

But these weren't the only books written that contained teachings and history that are very much like what we have in the Bible today. For example, during the first few centuries after Jesus' life here on earth, dozens of letters and other "gospels" were circulated in the Christian church.

So how do we know that all the books in the Bible are the ones God wanted? The answer lies in the great care He put into making sure all the words He inspired the biblical writers to record were kept in the book He has prepared and given us.

By the time of Jesus' birth, the collection of books included in the Hebrew Bible (the Old Testament) was pretty much decided. The Jewish people recognized that Moses,

### DID YOU KNOW...?
Moses and Jesus both spent part of their lives in Egypt!

# CHAPTER 1: HOW DID WE GET THIS BOOK ANYWAY?

the prophets, and other writers were God's messengers, so they accepted their work as the inspired Word of God. This collection is sometimes called the "canon of Scripture," and the act of declaring individual books as part of the Bible is called "canonization."

> **POWER WORDS**
> *Your word is a lamp to guide my feet and a light for my path.*
> Psalm 119:105

By the mid-third century AD, almost all Christian leaders agreed that the books we now have in the Old Testament belong in the canon of Scripture. But there was some disagreement about certain books that are not in the Bible but are part of what is called the Apocrypha (see the Did You Know. . .? sidebar on this page).

The process of accepting the New Testament books as part of the Bible began in the first century AD and continued on into the fourth century. By the beginning of the fourth century, Christians had already accepted most of the books now in the New Testament as God's Word. But a few books still needed final approval before they would be accepted as part of the canon.

Around AD 363, about 30 Christian leaders from what was then called Asia Minor (now part of the nation of Turkey) held a meeting called the Council of Laodicea. One of the things they talked about was the final acceptance of the canon of Scripture. This council decided that only the Old Testament, including the Apocrypha, and the 27 books in the New Testament could be read in the churches. Two other meetings—the Council of Hippo in AD 393 and the Council of Carthage in AD 397—also agreed that those same 27 books would be part of the New Testament.

# Same Message, Different Languages

> **DID YOU KNOW. . .?**
> Several books that are included in some Catholic versions of the Bible aren't found in other versions. The reason? These books are part of what is called the Apocrypha—which means "obscure," "hidden," or "secret." The books that make up the Apocrypha contain a lot of wisdom and historical teaching, but during the 1500s, during a time called the Protestant Reformation, they were taken out of the Bible for various reasons.

**Okay, now you** have a basic idea of how we got the books we have in the Bible today. But there is more to the story. Not only did God use some very brave people to record His words; He also used some very dedicated men to keep the original words in the Bible from being changed. That's why we can count on the fact that the message of the Bible is the same today as it was when it was first recorded thousands of years ago.

One thing that *has* changed is the languages people use. Very few people in the world today speak Hebrew or Greek, the languages used when the Bible was written. That means God's Word has had to be translated into languages that people could understand. God again used gifted and devoted

men to do His work, making it possible for people to read and understand the Bible in their own languages.

The translation of the Bible into other languages actually began even before Jesus was born. Starting around 285 BC, a group of 72 men began translating the Old Testament books from their original language of Hebrew into Greek—the common language that most people spoke back then. This translation was called the Septuagint.

The word *Septuagint* is Greek for 70, which approximates the number of translators who worked on the project. According to one story about this translation of the Hebrew Old Testament into Greek, it took the 72 translators 72 days to finish the project. But it actually took a lot longer than that!

The project was started because Ptolemy, the Egyptian king, wanted to include the literature of all the world's ancient religions in his library at Alexandria. Ptolemy contacted a man named Eleazar, the Jewish chief priest at the time, and asked him to assign Hebrew scholars from Jerusalem to work on the translation. Six men were chosen from each of the 12 tribes of Israel, which accounts for the 72 translators.

At first, they translated only the five books of the Old Testament, the Law of Moses; but after a while, they translated the other books and added them to the collection.

By the time Jesus was born, the Septuagint was read by most Greek-speaking Jews. It was also read in church gatherings during the first century AD—because the New Testament had not yet been completed, the first Christians didn't have it to read like we do now.

# The Bible in the "Common Language"

**Most of the** New Testament was originally written in Greek. But as the years passed, Latin replaced Greek as the language that most people spoke in the Roman Empire—which meant that someone would have to translate the New Testament into Latin.

That someone was Jerome, a church leader who lived from about AD 347 to 420.

Around AD 382, Pope Damasus I asked Jerome to translate both the Old Testament and the New Testament into Latin. Jerome used the Greek copies of scripture as his starting point. He began by translating the Gospels—Matthew, Mark, Luke, and John—and the Old Testament. Jerome finished his work around AD 400, and it came to be known as the Vulgate.

The Vulgate was used in the Christian—mostly Catholic—church from the 4th century to the 15th century. Even though the primary language of the people continued to change, there were no new official translations done during this time. That's mostly because the Catholic Church, which was very powerful at the time, wouldn't allow anyone to translate the Bible into the people's spoken and written languages. So only the pope and the priests, who learned to read and write in Latin, could read and understand the Bible.

That began to change when brave men such as John Wycliffe and William Tyndale risked everything—including their lives—to make sure that people could read the Bible for themselves.

### DID YOU KNOW...?

Even though there wasn't much Bible translation going on between the 4th and 15th centuries, some translations of the New Testament into the language of the Anglo-Saxons—an early form of English—began showing up late in the tenth century (the AD 900s).

DISCOVER THE BIBLE

# A Big Step toward an English-Language Bible

**John Wycliffe was** a Catholic priest who lived in England in the 1300s. Even though he was a Catholic, he believed—and said—some things that got him in trouble with the church. One of the things he believed was that every Christian should have the right to read the Bible without the interference of the church.

Wycliffe knew that the Roman Catholic Church wouldn't allow anyone to translate the Bible into the languages that the "common" spoke and read. But he was willing to risk trouble with the authorities, so he moved ahead with his plans to translate the Bible into English.

Wycliffe—and probably several of his closest friends—began their work by translating Jerome's Latin Vulgate into English. It is believed that Wycliffe translated the four Gospels himself and that he may have translated the entire New Testament. The work of translating the whole Bible into English wasn't finished until several years after Wycliffe died of a stroke in 1384.

Wycliffe's work was just the beginning when it came to translating the Bible into English. Another Englishman, William Tyndale, picked up where Wycliffe left off.

This is Merton College at Oxford University, where William Tydale attended college.

CHAPTER 1: HOW DID WE GET THIS BOOK ANYWAY?

# William Tyndale Gives His All

**William Tyndale was** an amazing man who attended college at Oxford University, one of England's best schools. By the time he graduated, he had mastered seven languages, including Greek and Hebrew. Because he knew those languages so well, he was able to read the Bible for himself—in its original languages.

Tyndale knew what he wanted to do more than anything else, and that was to translate the Bible into English so that even the most uneducated Englishman could read it for himself. But he also knew that the Catholic Church was against the idea and that working on translating the Bible into English could cost him everything—including his life.

At first, he asked the church authorities for permission to translate the Bible into English. But because the leaders of the church believed that only the pope and priests were educated enough to truly understand the Bible, the answer was a big no!

Still, Tyndale wouldn't stop talking about how he disagreed with the church about many subjects, including translating the Bible into English. He began his translation work while he was still in England; but when the authorities found out what he was doing, he had to leave England. He traveled to Germany, where he could continue his work.

### DID YOU KNOW...?

It took a lot of courage for William Tyndale to work on translating the Bible into English. As an example of how brave he really was, consider this story: One day, Tyndale shouted at an English bishop who told him that the common people didn't need to read the Bible but only needed to listen to the words of the pope. "I defy the pope and all his laws!" Tyndale said. "And, if God spares me, I will one day make the boy that drives the plow in England to know more of the scriptures than the pope does!"

DISCOVER THE BIBLE

## Who, What, Where?

Even though he never worked on translating the Bible, a German inventor named Johannes Gutenberg played a huge part in making the Bible available to all people. Gutenberg developed the movable type printing press, which made it possible to mass-produce printed materials—including the Bible. In fact, the world's first printed book was the *Gutenberg Bible*, a 1,286-page printed version of the Latin Vulgate that came off the presses in the 1450s.

## Did You Know. . . ?

By the time William Tyndale arrived in Germany, a man named Martin Luther had already begun translating the Bible into the German language. In 1523, Luther published the first five books of the Bible in German. By the 1530s, he had published the entire Bible in German.

Translating the Bible into English was no easy job, and it took Tyndale more than a year just to complete the New Testament. After he finished, he and some of his friends arranged for the English Bibles to be smuggled into England. The people loved the "new" Bibles, but the authorities weren't impressed. They made plans to stop Tyndale for good.

Tyndale knew he could not return home to England. He loved his native land and missed his friends and family there, but he knew that going home would mean almost certain death. Instead, he left Germany and traveled to Antwerp, Belgium, where, in 1530, his translation of the first five books of the Old Testament was printed. He also planned to translate the remainder of the Old Testament.

Tyndale didn't live long enough to realize his dream of an English translation of the entire Bible. In May 1535, he was arrested in Antwerp and thrown in a prison cell. Later that year, he was executed.

## Finishing What William Tyndale Started

**After William Tyndale's** death, one of his friends, a man named Miles Coverdale, completed the translation of the Old Testament. In 1535, Coverdale printed the first complete Bible in the English language. It was called the Coverdale Bible. Two years after that, John Rogers, another friend of Tyndale's, printed the second complete English Bible. He translated his Bible directly from Hebrew and Greek manuscripts. It was called Matthew's Bible.

In 1539, Coverdale published what is now known as the Great Bible (it is called that because it was really big—about 14 inches thick). Even though the "common" people still weren't allowed to own copies of the Bible or to read the Bible on their own, the Great Bible brought English Christians a step closer.

## The King James Bible—the World's Number 1 Bestseller

**In 1604, King** James I of England appointed 54 of the world's best Bible scholars and language experts of the time to translate the Bible into English. Each of these men knew the Hebrew, Greek, and Aramaic languages well. It wasn't easy work, and it took several years to finish it. Their final product came to be known as the King James Bible (also known as the Authorized Version), and it was completed and printed in 1611.

At first, the people of England—and other English-speaking places—didn't like the King James Bible as much as other translations. They preferred the Geneva Bible, an English translation that had been around for several decades. But in time, the King James Bible became more and more popular. Eventually, it became the world's all-time bestselling book. By the end of the 18th century, the King James Bible had become the only Bible used in English-speaking Protestant (non-Catholic) churches.

## Look How Far We've Come!

**You're fortunate enough** to live in a time when you can walk into any bookstore and buy your own copy of the Bible. Not only that, but you can buy one of literally dozens of translations. All you have to do is find one that is easy for you to read and understand, plunk down your money, and take home your very own Bible.

Translation of the Bible didn't stop with the King James Bible. Since the King James Bible was first printed and distributed in 1611, Bible translators have worked tirelessly through the years to adapt the language of the Bible—while keeping the content the same.

> **POWER WORDS**
>
> *"People are like grass; their beauty is like a flower in the field. The grass withers and the flower fades. But the word of the Lord remains forever."*
>
> 1 Peter 1:24-25

## DISCOVER THE BIBLE

Here are some of the versions translators have produced since the King James Bible first came on the scene:

- 1885—The English Revised Version, the first major revision of the King James Bible
- 1900–01—The American publishing company Thomas Nelson & Sons publishes the American Standard Version
- 1952—The Revised Standard Version
- 1965—The Amplified Bible
- 1971—The New American Standard Bible and *The Living Bible* (a paraphrase)
- 1976—*The Good News Bible*
- 1978—The New International Version
- 1982—The complete New King James Version
- 1989—The New Revised Standard Version
- 1995—The Contemporary English Version
- 1996—The New Living Translation
- 2001—The English Standard Version
- 2002—*The Message* (a paraphrase)
- 2004—The Holman Christian Standard Bible

With all these versions of the Bible—and many others—around, it's hard to believe there was a time when ordinary people weren't even allowed to *read* the Bible themselves, let alone own one. But it's true.

We can be grateful that God used so many people to put His thoughts and deeds down on paper, and then to make the Bible available to anyone who wants one.

As you're starting to see, the Bible really is an amazing book. . .and the God who gave it to you really is an awesome God!

# CHAPTER 2

## In the Beginning... and Beyond

How It All Started (Genesis through Deuteronomy)

**The Bible begins** with five books that, as a group, are called the Pentateuch. The word *Pentateuch* is a Greek word that means "five rolls" or "five cases." Jewish people call the first five books of the Bible the *Torah*.

The first five books of the Old Testament are a set of books about beginnings—the beginnings of the universe and the world around us, the beginning of the human race, the beginning of God's plan for the salvation of humankind, the beginning of the Hebrew people and the nation of Israel, and the beginning of God's rules, laws, and guidelines for living.

By the time you finish reading those five books—Genesis through Deuteronomy—you will have read everything the Bible says about human history, starting with Adam and Eve and ending with the death of Moses.

Does that sound like fun reading?
Let's get started!

## Genesis

**What It's About:** The word *genesis* means "beginnings," and that's what the book of Genesis is all about. This book is about the *beginning* of the universe and the world around us, the *beginning* of life, the *beginning* of the human race, the *beginning* of sin, and the *beginning* of a special race of people through whom God chose and prepared to bring salvation to the world.

DISCOVER THE BIBLE

**Important Characters/People:** Adam and Eve, Noah, Abraham, Sarah, Lot, Isaac, Rebekah, Jacob, Esau, Joseph, Potiphar, Pharaoh

Adam and Eve

Noah

Abraham and Sarah

Jacob and Esau

Joseph

**The Writer:** None of the first five books of the Bible names its writer, but many centuries of tradition say that Moses wrote all of them. Moses lived around the 1400s BC.

# What You'll Find in the Book of Genesis

**Knowing what the** word *genesis* means, doesn't it make sense that the book of Genesis begins with the words "In the beginning"? This was the moment when God began the miraculous six-day process of creating everything you see around you—the universe, our solar system, our planet, and every living thing that inhabits the earth.

The first two chapters of Genesis give us a bare-bones outline of what God created and when He created it. You won't find a lot of detail about the process of creation in Genesis—or anywhere else in the Bible, for that matter. How God did it remains a mystery. But as someone once wisely said, "I don't know *how* God did it; I just believe Him when He says, 'In the beginning, God created. . .'"

CHAPTER 2: IN THE BEGINNING. . .AND BEYOND

Genesis 1 divides the process into six days of creation. On the first day, God laid the groundwork for all life on earth when He created light. Without light—light from the sun, that is—nothing could live, grow, or reproduce here on earth. Here is a basic list of what God created on each creation day:

Day 1: The earth itself and light (1:2–5)
Day 2: The sky and the oceans (1:6–8)
Day 3: Dry land and plants (1:9–13)
Day 4: The sun, moon, and stars (1:14–19)
Day 5: Birds and fish (1:20–23)
Day 6: Other animals. . .and people! (1:24–31)

When God finished the job of creation, He looked at everything He had done and "saw that it was very good" (Genesis 1:31). God had just made *paradise*, and He told Adam and Eve, the world's first two humans, to reproduce and to care for His creation.

Everything was perfect, *until. . .*!

## It Was All Downhill from Here

**The third chapter** of Genesis tells us that the serpent—actually the devil in the guise of a snake—deceived Adam and Eve and got them to do the one thing God had told them not to do: eat from the tree of the knowledge of good and evil. And when they did that, they brought on another beginning from the book of Genesis: the beginning of sin.

From that moment on, it was all downhill for the human race. Adam and Eve were kicked out of the Garden of Eden. Genesis 4 reports how jealousy, anger, and even murder became a part of human life. And as the years went on, things only got worse. In fact, things got so bad that God decided to scrap the whole thing and start over.

### DID YOU KNOW. . .?

The Old Testament is filled with what are called "messianic prophecies"—predictions of the coming Messiah, Jesus Christ. The first prophecy is found in Genesis 3:15, where God says to the serpent (Satan), "I will cause hostility between you and the woman, and between your offspring and her offspring. He will strike your head, and you will strike his heel." This meant that the Messiah would be born from a woman and that He would one day destroy the devil.

DISCOVER THE BIBLE

## Water, Water Everywhere—the Flood

**You've probably read** or heard the story of Noah (Genesis 6–9). Several hundred years after God kicked Adam and Eve out of Eden, humans had become so sinful and violent that God decided to send a huge flood to destroy the whole human race—except for Noah and his family.

God told Noah to build a huge boat called an ark. The plan was for Noah, his family, and some of each kind of animal to get in the ark before the rains came and stay there until dry land appeared again. Five months after the flood started, the ark came to rest on a mountain called Ararat. A few months later, more land started to appear. Several more months later, Noah and his family—along with all those animals—left the ark and began repopulating the earth all over again.

CHAPTER 2: IN THE BEGINNING. . .AND BEYOND

## Abraham and Some Other Biblical "Fathers"

**The book of** Genesis shifts gears in chapter 12. While the first 11 chapters tell us the story of the beginnings of the universe and of human history, chapter 12 is the start of what is called *patriarchal history*.

The word *patriarch* is kind of a fancy name for "father." The four patriarchs of the book of Genesis are Abraham (Genesis 12–25:8), Isaac (21:1–35), Jacob (Genesis 25:21–50:14), and Joseph (Genesis 30:22–50:26). When you call these men patriarchs, what you're really saying is that they are fathers of the nation of Israel.

There are a lot of important characters in the book of Genesis, but probably the most important is Abraham, the man God chose to be the father of the Hebrew nation. You can read all about Abraham (or Abram, as he was called earlier in his life before God gave him a new name) in Genesis 12–24.

Even though Abraham wasn't a perfect man—he made more than his share of mistakes—he was still a man who believed that God kept His promises. That made a difference in nearly everything Abraham did!

When you first start reading about the patriarch Abraham, you may wonder if someone misspelled his name in the first few chapters that tell his amazing life story. But the name *Abram* is not a typo. Abram and Abraham are the same guy. After God called Abram and told him to move to Canaan, He promised Abram he'd be the father of a great nation and a blessing to the entire world.

Abraham (we'll use this name from now on to avoid further confusion) is first mentioned in Genesis 11; but it's in chapter 12 where his life gets really interesting. Abraham was 75 years old when God told him to leave Ur and travel to Canaan. But he never questioned God—he just did what he was told.

It probably helped that God made him an amazing promise: "I will make you a great nation; I will bless you and make your name great; and you shall be a blessing. I will bless those who bless you, and I will curse him who curses you; and in you all the families of the earth shall be blessed" (Genesis 12:2–3 NKJV).

### WHO, WHAT, WHERE?

Ur was a place—probably a large city—located in what is now Iraq, about 600 miles east of Canaan, which is the land in and around Israel today. Ur was the birthplace of Abraham and Haran, his brother. Abraham and his family lived in Ur before God commanded him to travel to Canaan.

23

DISCOVER THE BIBLE

# The Promise of a Son...and Millions of Family Members

### POWER WORDS

*And Abram believed the LORD, and the LORD counted him as righteous because of his faith.*
Genesis 15:6

### WHAT'S IN IT FOR ME?

The story of Isaac's birth is a good reminder of two things: God always keeps His promises, even when it doesn't seem humanly possible; and we need to wait patiently—sometimes for years—for God to keep His promises. You can never go wrong when you simply trust God to do what He says He will do.

**Later, as you** can read in Genesis 17, God repeated His promise to Abraham, only this time He was a little more specific. God promised Abraham that He would begin a new race of people through him and his wife, Sarah—even though Abraham was 99 years old and Sarah was way too old to have children. God promised He would make Abraham the father of many nations and that he would have millions of descendants. This is when God renamed him Abraham and renamed his wife Sarah as well (she was called Sarai before that).

In time—after Abraham and Sarah hatched a plan to produce a son through Sarah's servant, Hagar (you can read this story in Genesis 16)—God kept His promise. Genesis 17 says that Sarah became pregnant and gave birth to the son God had promised them. They named him Isaac, as God had told them to, and he later became the founder of the nation God had promised Abraham and his family.

## This Is Only a Test...

**Abraham knew beyond** all doubt that his son Isaac was the result of God's keeping His promises. But one day, Abraham had to wonder what God could possibly be thinking when He told Abraham to do the unthinkable: sacrifice Isaac on an altar.

Genesis 22 tells the story of Abraham hearing that command and then obediently taking Isaac to a place called Moriah, where he built an altar and prepared to take his son's life. Abraham had placed Isaac on top of the altar, and was about to sacrifice him, when an angel of the Lord stopped him and told him not to harm the young man.

In the end, Abraham sacrificed a ram—caught by its horns in a thicket—instead of his son Isaac.

CHAPTER 2: IN THE BEGINNING. . .AND BEYOND

It was all a test. God wanted Abraham to discover just how deeply he trusted God and just how committed he was to obeying God's every command. Because Abraham proved how faithful he was, God again promised to bless Abraham with countless millions of descendants—all of whom would also be descendants of his son Isaac.

## More Branches on the Family Tree

**After the death** of Sarah, Abraham arranged a marriage for Isaac. He sent a servant to his brother Nahor's home to find a wife for Isaac. The servant returned with Nahor's daughter Rebekah. Isaac married Rebekah, and after much prayer—because Rebekah at first couldn't get pregnant—she had twin sons: Esau and Jacob.

Esau was Isaac's favorite son, but when Isaac was very old, Jacob tricked his blind father into giving him the blessing meant for the firstborn child in that culture. (You can read this story in Genesis 27.) That meant that Jacob, not Esau, would become the forefather of the Hebrew people.

Later, Jacob himself was tricked into marrying a woman named Leah—when he really wanted to marry her sister, Rachel. In those days, men were allowed to have more than one wife, so he also married Rachel. Jacob, whom God renamed Israel, became the father of 12 sons, and his family came to be known as the 12 tribes of Israel.

One of those sons was named Joseph, and his story takes up the last 20 chapters of the book of Genesis.

### FUN BIBLE TRIVIA

The book of Genesis doesn't say what Abraham was thinking as he prepared to sacrifice his son Isaac, but in the New Testament, the book of Hebrews suggests that Abraham believed that if he had actually slain his son, God would have raised Isaac from the dead. (You can look it up in Hebrews 11:17–19.)

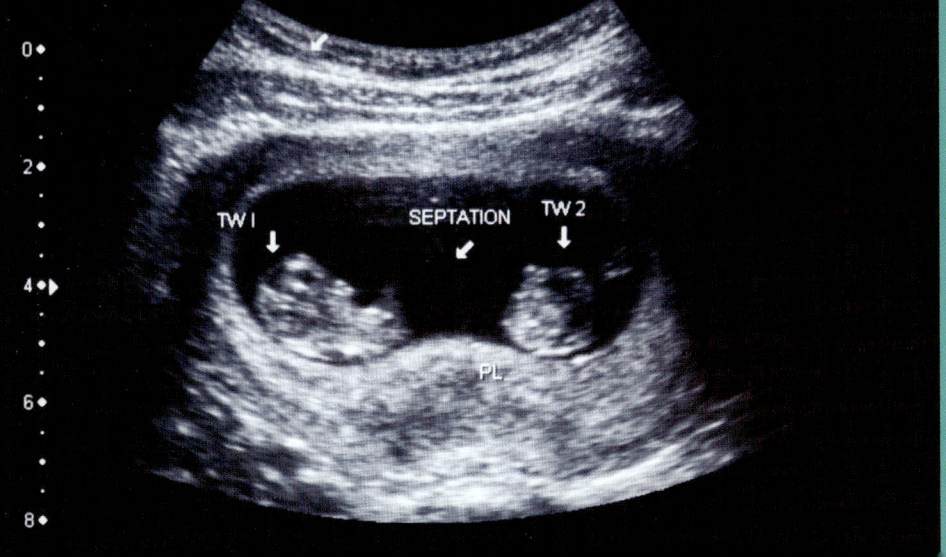

Modern technology allows us to see twins in their mother's womb—but Jacob and Esau were born 4,000 years before ultrasounds!

### DID YOU KNOW. . .?

The name Jacob means "supplanter," which is another word for someone who replaces someone, often by trickery or force. This makes sense, because Jacob—with the help of his mother—tricked his father into giving him a birthright meant for his older brother, Esau. Though God doesn't approve of trickery and deception, Jacob's story is an example of how God uses imperfect people to carry out His perfect plans.

DISCOVER THE BIBLE

## That's Some Jacket You're Wearing, Joseph!

**Joseph was the** second-youngest of 12 sons born to Jacob. You can only imagine the kind of problems he faced being one of 12 boys, but to make matters worse, he was Jacob's favorite, which made the other brothers mad. Not only that, Joseph was a bit of a tattletale, who brought his father bad reports of some of the things the other boys were doing. To top it off, Jacob set Joseph apart by giving him a beautiful robe (called a "coat of many colors" in some Bible versions).

When Joseph's 10 older brothers saw the robe their father had given Joseph, they became very jealous. They disliked him so much that they wouldn't even say anything nice to him. Things only got worse for Joseph when he told his brothers about a couple of strange dreams he had—both of which showed him that his brothers would bow down to him.

A few days later, Jacob asked Joseph to check up on his brothers, who were working in the fields. When the brothers saw him coming, they made plans to kill him. But Reuben, the eldest brother, had another idea: he said they should just throw Joseph into a well and leave him there to die. (Reuben's real plan was to come back later by himself and rescue Joseph.)

After the brothers stripped off Joseph's coat and tossed him into the empty well, a group of men came by on their way to Egypt. That gave Judah, another one of the brothers, an idea. Why not sell Joseph to the men as a slave? That way, the brothers would be innocent of killing him—and they would make a nice profit besides!

So Joseph was off to Egypt, where he was sold to an important man named Potiphar. Meanwhile, Joseph's brothers dipped Joseph's robe in animal blood and took it to Jacob, who believed a wild animal had killed his favorite son.

Joseph started out his life in Egypt as a slave, but because he was faithful to God—and because God blessed him—Joseph became an important person in Egypt. He even got to talk to Pharaoh himself and told him the meaning of some of his dreams.

### WHAT'S IN IT FOR ME?

When you read about how Joseph's brothers treated him—how they sold him to a bunch of strangers—you might be tempted to say, "That's not fair!" But keep in mind that God used what happened to Joseph to help keep the Hebrew race from starving to death. Joseph is an example of how God can use everything that happens in your life—even the tough times you have to go through—for your own good.

CHAPTER 2: IN THE BEGINNING...AND BEYOND

One of those dreams meant that there would be a terrible time in the surrounding world when people wouldn't have any food to eat. So Joseph advised Pharaoh to save up lots of food during the good times, so people wouldn't starve to death later.

When the hard times came, people came from all over to buy grain from Joseph. That included Joseph's brothers, who bowed to him—just as he had told them they would—because he was such an important person.

Joseph had the authority to have his brothers punished—even put to death—for what they had done to him. But he wasn't about to do that. Instead, he told them not to be afraid of him or angry at themselves for selling him, because God had used what they had done to keep a lot of people from dying.

So Jacob, Joseph's brothers, and their families left Canaan and moved to Egypt to live with Joseph. They had all the food they needed, and their families got bigger and bigger. Because they were Joseph's family, they had the best of everything.

Joseph died in Egypt at the age of 110. But before he died, he promised his brothers that God would one day rescue them and take them back to Canaan. The book of Genesis ends with Joseph's body being placed in a coffin in Egypt.

Now it's time to look ahead about four centuries to see what became of Joseph's descendants in Egypt—and how God made good on Joseph's promise.

# Exodus

**What It's About:** The word *exodus* literally means "departure," and that's what the story in the book of Exodus is all about. The book of Genesis ends with Abraham's descendants living in Egypt as guests of Joseph. After spending more than four hundred years in Egypt, the Hebrews—by now, hundreds of thousands of families—were living in a foreign land as slaves. That all changed when God assigned His own chosen man, Moses, to bring the people of Israel out of Egyptian slavery and set them on their way to the Promised Land of Canaan.

**Important Characters/People:** Moses, Aaron, Miriam, Pharaoh, Jethro, Joshua

**The Writer:** Moses (see page 20)

27

DISCOVER THE BIBLE

Egyptian taskmasters whip their Hebrew slaves.

# What You'll Find in the Book of Exodus

**The Israelites had** it pretty good in Egypt while Joseph was alive. But after Joseph died, the new pharaoh saw the tribes of Israel not as welcome guests but as a threat to his nation. So Pharaoh made the Israelites slaves in Egypt. God saw what was happening to His chosen people, and He heard their cries for a deliverer. So He called a shepherd named Moses to lead them out of slavery in Egypt.

At first, Moses wasn't sure he was the man for the job. Even though God appeared to him in a miraculous way—out of a bush that looked like it was on fire, even though it wasn't burned up—Moses made excuses about why he couldn't lead the Hebrews out of Egypt. (You can read this story in Exodus 3–4.)

# CHAPTER 2: IN THE BEGINNING. . .AND BEYOND

But God wasn't going to have it any other way. Eventually, He convinced Moses that he was the right person to lead the Hebrews, and Moses went to Pharaoh with this demand: "Let my people go!" (Exodus 5:1).

Pharaoh knew he had a good thing going with all the free labor provided by the Hebrew slaves, and he wasn't about to let them just walk away—at least not without some heavy persuasion from above! Chapters 7–12 of Exodus tell the story of a series of 10 plagues that God sent on Egypt because Pharaoh wouldn't let the Hebrew nation go free. First it was the water in the Nile River turning to blood, then plagues of frogs, gnats, and flies. Then came the death of the livestock in Egypt, boils breaking out on the people, hail, locusts, and three days of darkness.

Still, Pharaoh wouldn't budge—not until God sent the final plague: the death of all firstborn male children in Egypt. When Pharaoh saw what had happened, he *begged* Moses and his people to leave Egypt for good. The Egyptian people wanted the Hebrews to leave so much that they let them take anything they wanted with them—as long as they left right away!

> **POWER WORDS**
> 
> *God replied to Moses, "I Am Who I Am. Say this to the people of Israel: I Am has sent me to you."*
> 
> Exodus 3:14

> **WHO, WHAT, WHERE?**
> 
> Where would Moses have been without his big brother, Aaron? When Moses complained that he wasn't a very good speaker, God appointed Aaron as Moses' spokesman, a position he held for almost 40 years. Aaron was also the first priest of Israel and the father of a line of priests that continued for more than 1,000 years.

29

DISCOVER THE BIBLE

## Time to Hit the Road…for the Promised Land!

**What a sight** it must have been! Hundreds of thousands of people gathering for their exodus from Egypt!

Even though the people of Israel were beginning a journey to the Promised Land, they didn't take the shortest way there—which would have been a straight line through the desert. Instead, they headed toward a place called the Wilderness of Sinai, which is located near the southern tip of the Sinai Peninsula. It was here that God called Moses to the top of Mount Sinai to give him rules to govern the Hebrew people, including the Ten Commandments.

## A Mountaintop Experience, the Laws of God…and a Calf Made of Gold

### FUN BIBLE TRIVIA

Ever wonder where in the Bible you can find the Ten Commandments? They're found in Exodus 20:3–17. How many of the Ten Commandments can you remember? Write down the ones that come to mind, and then look them up in your Bible to see how many you got right and how many you missed.

**Moses' time with** God on the mountain wasn't just a quick visit. In fact, his visit with God is covered in chapters 20–32 of Exodus. The people expected Moses to be back in a short time, and after a while they started to think he had died on the mountain. The people lost their patience and pressured Aaron into building them a golden idol in the shape of a calf.

When Moses returned to the camp and saw the idol, he became so angry that he smashed the stone tablets of the Law. After the idol was destroyed (and after God had restored order), God called Moses back to the mountain and gave him a new copy of the Law.

The last six chapters of Exodus tell the story of the Hebrews' continued journey toward the Promised Land, and the construction of the tabernacle, a movable tent used for service and worship to God.

CHAPTER 2: IN THE BEGINNING. . .AND BEYOND

# Leviticus

**What It's About:** Once God had delivered the people of Israel out of slavery in Egypt, He instructed them how to live and how to worship Him. That included a system of sacrifices that would one day be replaced by the onetime sacrifice of Jesus Christ on the cross.

**Important Characters/People:** Moses, Aaron, Nadab, Abihu, Ithamar, Eleazar

**The Writer:** Moses (see page 20)

# What You'll Find in the Book of Leviticus

The people of Israel lived as slaves in Egypt for more than 400 years. As a result of living among a people that worshipped many false gods, the way the Hebrews viewed God was warped. The words recorded in the book of Leviticus are the words of a God who wanted to bring His people back into fellowship with Him.

The people of Israel were imperfect—just like everyone else—but they were *God's* people, and He provided the words recorded in Leviticus to give them instructions on how to have a relationship with a holy God. That's why you'll see the word *holy* throughout the book of Leviticus. God is holy, and He wants His people to be holy, too. And in those days, the only way for that to happen was through sacrifices to pay for the people's sins.

The first seven chapters of Leviticus cover the various offerings and sacrifices that God required from the people. The first three chapters are about what are called *voluntary offerings*, which were meant as worship to God.

God *hated* it when His people worshipped silly idols!

### POWER WORDS

*"For I am the Lord your God. You must consecrate yourselves and be holy, because I am holy."*

Leviticus 11:44

31

## DISCOVER THE BIBLE

### WHAT'S IN IT FOR ME?

Christians don't live under the rules listed in the book of Leviticus. So why should we read this book? When we read Leviticus, we are reminded of what Jesus has done for us! Because Jesus died for us, we no longer have to offer any of the sacrifices listed in this book, because Jesus has paid the price once and for all for our sins.

Chapters 4 and 5 address offerings made to cover people's sins. Chapters 6 and 7 record laws and regulations about the different kinds of offerings.

Chapters 8–10 cover the rules and regulations for the priesthood of that time. Chapters 11–16 explain to the Hebrew people what to do in order to deal with different kinds of "uncleanness." The last 10 chapters are instructions and guidelines for holy living.

# Numbers

**What It's About:** Even though God brought the nation of Israel out of slavery in Egypt—and performed some amazing miracles for everyone to see—the people were ungrateful and unbelieving. As a result, they were forced to wander in the wilderness of Sinai for 40 years.

**Important Characters/People:** Moses, Aaron, Joshua, Balaam, Eleazar, the 70 elders, Caleb, Korah, Dathan, Abiram, the 12 spies, Gad, Reuben

**The Writer:** Moses (see page 20)

## What You'll Find in the Book of Numbers

**At the beginning** of the book of Numbers, God instructs Moses to count all the young men of Israel—which is how the book got its name. God told Moses and his brother, Aaron, along with leaders of the 12 tribes, to do the counting.

### POWER WORDS

"And if the Lord is pleased with us, he will bring us safely into that land and give it to us. It is a rich land flowing with milk and honey."

Numbers 14:8

# CHAPTER 2: IN THE BEGINNING. . .AND BEYOND

Most of the events in the book of Numbers take place in the wilderness between Egypt and Canaan. The book begins 14 months after the people had left Egypt, and long after they should have entered the Promised Land. But even though they should have completed the journey in less than two weeks, they were still decades away from claiming the land that God had promised to give them. That's because God was punishing them for their constant complaining and rebellion.

The book of Numbers includes probably the best—or the worst—example of the people's rebellion and lack of faith. It happened while the people were camped out at a place called Kadesh, which was located in the Desert of Zin. They were just days away from entering the Promised Land when Moses sent representatives from each of Israel's 12 tribes ahead to check out the land. When they returned, they told the people that everything they had been told about the land was true and that it would be a great place to live and raise their families.

So what was the problem?

Two of the spies—Joshua and Caleb—told the people to get ready to take the land and that there was no way they could fail, because God would be with them. But 10 of the spies told the people about giants living in the land—giants so big that they made the men of Israel look like grasshoppers in comparison.

Sadly, the people of Israel chose to listen to the 10—and they rebelled against Moses and against God and refused to move out to take the land. Because they rebelled, and because they failed to believe God, many of them died at Kadesh. (You can read the whole story in Numbers 13–14.)

Sadly, a whole generation of people who were just days away from enjoying life in a land flowing with milk and honey instead died in the wilderness. Moses had prayed to God for the rebellious people, and God forgave them. But He wasn't going to reward them for their lack of faith

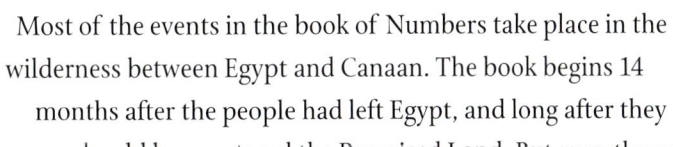

Moses sent 12 men to "spy out" the Promised Land.

### WHO, WHAT, WHERE?

Caleb, who was a member of the tribe of Judah, was one of the 12 spies Moses sent to spy out the land of Canaan. He is an example of what can happen in the life of someone who trusts God instead of allowing fear to rule. The Bible says that Caleb trusted God and acted on that trust, so he became an example of the kind of faith God honors and rewards (see Joshua 14:6–15). Do you have that kind of faith in God?

## DISCOVER THE BIBLE

### WHAT'S IN IT FOR ME?

It's not pleasant reading about thousands of people dying in a desert because they refused to believe God but instead focused on a bunch of giants. But the story of what happened at Kadesh is a great reminder to focus on the size of our God and not on the size of the giants in your life. When you do that, you'll be more than willing to do exactly what God asks you to do—and you'll enjoy the good things God has for you as a result!

Ten of the 12 spies said they didn't want to face the giants in the Promised Land!

and obedience. They would have to wander in the wilderness until everyone over the age of 20 had died.

Even Moses wasn't allowed to enter the Promised Land. But Joshua and Caleb, the two spies who had tried their best to rally the people and get them to claim what God had already given them, were allowed to enter the land of Canaan.

# Deuteronomy

**What It's About:** Moses, who had led Israel out of captivity and slavery in Egypt, speaks to the Hebrew people four times to remind them where they had come from, where they had been, whom they belonged to (God), and how belonging to God should affect their lives.

**Important Characters/People:** Moses, Joshua, the Canaanites, the Hittites, the Girgashites, the Amorites, the Perizzites, the Hivites, the Jebusites

**The Writer:** Moses (See page 20)

CHAPTER 2: IN THE BEGINNING. . .AND BEYOND

# What You'll Find in the Book of Deuteronomy

**Chapters 1–4** of Deuteronomy record Moses' words to his people reminding them of their 40 years in the wilderness. Moses didn't talk to the people about that time just to give them a history lesson. He wanted them to remember *why* they had wandered in the wilderness—because of their disobedience and lack of faith.

In chapters 5–11, you can read about how Moses repeated the Ten Commandments (5:6–21), reminded the people of the importance of doing what God had told them to do, and promised the people they would soon enter the Promised Land.

Moses begins this part of his address by telling the people, "Listen carefully, Israel. Hear the decrees and regulations I am giving you today, so you may learn them and obey them!" (5:1).

## WHAT'S IN IT FOR ME?

God promises that when you come to Him to confess your sin, He will completely forgive you and cleanse you. It's true now, and it was true in the days of Moses. So why would Moses remind the people of what they had done wrong after they left Egypt? So they would remember their mistakes and not make the same ones again! When you think about the things you've done that displease God, don't beat yourself up. Instead, thank God for His forgiveness. . .and for the lessons He has taught you when you made bad decisions.

The book of Deuteronomy is a written record of Moses' spoken sermons to God's people.

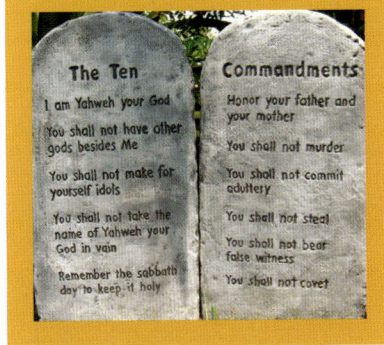

## POWER WORDS

"And you must love the Lord your God with all your heart, all your soul, and all your strength."

Deuteronomy 6:5

35

DISCOVER THE BIBLE

Moses sees the Promised Land from far away, in a 19th-century painting by James Joseph Jacques Tissot.

In chapters 12–26, Moses reminds the Hebrews of the laws and rules that God wants them to obey once they enter the Promised Land. In chapters 27–30, he tells them what kinds of blessings they would receive for obeying those laws.

Chapters 31–33 are Moses' final words to the people before his death—his final good-byes. Chapter 34 is the account of Moses' final days, which he spent on Mount Nebo on the plains of Moab. From there, God showed him the Promised Land, which the people of Israel would soon enter.

After Moses' death, Joshua—the same Joshua who years before had so bravely tried to encourage the people of Israel to possess the land—took over as leader of the Hebrew people.

That's what you'll read about in the next chapter!

# CHAPTER 3

# His Story... and Their Story

**The History of God's People (Joshua through Esther)**

**Someone once said** that the Bible isn't just history, but that it's "His story," meaning the story of how God relates to the human race.

The first five books of the Bible—the collection called the Pentateuch—are books about beginnings and the Law of Moses. The next 12 are books of history, and they're the ones that tell the story of the rise and fall, and then the rise again, of the nation of Israel.

These books of history cover more than 1,000 years, starting with the appointment of Joshua to lead the Israelites into the Promised Land (around 1452 BC) and ending after the return of the Jews to Israel following what is called the Babylonian Captivity (which you'll read about later in this chapter).

The people of Israel enjoyed some good times during this period, but they also went through some bad times. As you'll see in this chapter—and in the books of the Bible it covers—those bad times happened because of some bad decisions on the part of Israel's leaders and on the part of the people.

As you read through this part of the Bible, you'll learn how the people of Israel moved into the Promised Land, how they became a kingdom with a human king, how Israel was divided into two kingdoms called Judah and Israel, and the good and bad (mostly bad) things the kings who ruled over Judah and Israel did during their reigns.

DISCOVER THE BIBLE

# Joshua

**What It's About:** After wandering in the wilderness for 40 years, the people of Israel—now led by Joshua—capture and settle the Promised Land, also known as the land of Canaan.

**Important Characters/People:** Joshua, Caleb, Rahab, Eleazar, Achan

**The Writer:** The book of Joshua doesn't name its writer, but most experts agree that Joshua himself wrote most of it. (The last five verses describe Joshua's death and legacy, so someone else would have written those verses.)

### POWER WORDS

*"This is my command—be strong and courageous! Do not be afraid or discouraged. For the LORD your God is with you wherever you go."*

Joshua 1:9

## What You'll Find in the Book of Joshua

**This book picks** up where the book of Deuteronomy leaves off. Moses has died, and now it's up to Joshua the "son of Nun" (1:1) to finish what Moses started and lead the people of Israel into the Promised Land. Before his death, Moses appointed Joshua as the new leader of the Hebrews (see Deuteronomy 34:9). As the book of Joshua begins, God gives Joshua the encouragement and command to "be strong and courageous" (Joshua 1:6, 7, 9). Almost all of the rebellious people who had earlier lost out on their chance to enter the Promised Land have died, leaving a group of people who are ready to follow Joshua's lead and take what God had already said was theirs.

CHAPTER 3: HIS STORY. . .AND THEIR STORY

The book of Joshua is split into two 12-chapter sections. The first 12 chapters tell the story of the Israelites' conquest of the people and armies that stood in their way; the last 12 chapters tell the story of how the Israelites divided the land of Canaan among the 12 tribes of Israel. The city of Jericho is the Israelites' first major obstacle under Joshua's leadership. But God demonstrates what He can do when His people obey His commands. God commanded Joshua's army to march outside Jericho. . .blowing trumpets and shouting! When they did that, God knocked the city walls flat, and the Israelites defeated the city. After that, Joshua's armies drove idol-worshipping people such as the Hittites, Amorites, Canaanites, Perizzites, Hivites, and Jebusites from Canaan.

### FUN BIBLE TRIVIA

Joshua is a Hebrew name that means either "Jehovah is his help," "Jehovah the Savior," or "Jehovah is salvation." The name *Jesus* essentially means the very same thing!

### WHO, WHAT, WHERE?

Rahab was a woman in Jericho who played a big part in the Israelites' defeat of the city. When Joshua sent two spies to check out the city before Israel attacked it, Rahab hid them from the king of Jericho. In return for her kindness, the men promised she and her family would be spared if she hung a scarlet cord from her window when Israel attacked. Rahab is mentioned in the New Testament as a woman of great faith (Hebrews 11:31; James 2:25). You can read the story of Rahab in Joshua 2:1–24.

DISCOVER THE BIBLE

# Judges

**What It's About:** Judges is a book of ups and downs—followed by still more ups and downs. It tells the 350-year story of how the people of Israel strayed away from God, the punishment the people suffered as a result, and their turning back to God. Each time Israel abandoned God, He appointed leaders, called judges, to lead them back to Him.

**Important Characters/People:** Othniel, Ehud, Shamgar, Deborah, Gideon, Abimelech, Tola, Jair, Jephthah, Ibzan, Elon, Abdon, Samson, Barak, Jael, Micah, the Midianites, the Amalekites, the Philistines, the Ammonites

**The Writer:** Experts aren't certain who wrote the book of Judges, but most believe it was the prophet Samuel.

### FUN BIBLE TRIVIA

Some of the Judges listed in the book of Judges had very unusual families. For example, Jair had 30 sons (10:4) and Abdon had 40 sons (12:14). Ibzan had 30 sons and 30 daughters (12:9). Jephthah, on the other hand, had only one child, a daughter he foolishly vowed to sacrifice to God in exchange for a military victory (11:30–40).

## What You'll Find in the Book of Judges

**This book picks** up not long after the book of Joshua leaves off. It tells the stories of 13 people—12 men and one woman—who lead the nation of Israel against the enemies who took over because of the Israelites' disobedience.

The stories in the book of Judges aren't pleasant ones. You can read about how the nation of Israel spent almost four centuries falling away from God, suffering the consequences, and then being rescued by one of the 13 judges.

These are the 13 judges listed in this book and where you can read about them:

**Othniel (Judges 3:7–11)**—Caleb's brother, who delivered Israel from the king of Mesopotamia and judged Israel for 40 years.

Jair had 30 sons who rode 30 donkeys.

# CHAPTER 3: HIS STORY...AND THEIR STORY

**Ehud (Judges 3:12–30)**—He defeated the oppressing Moabites. Ehud killed Eglon, the king of Moab, with a dagger while pretending to be on a peace mission.

**Shamgar (Judges 3:31)**—He fought bravely against the Philistines, killing 600 soldiers with an ox goad—a pointed rod used to prod along oxen as they pulled a cart.

**Deborah (Judges 4–5)**—She was Israel's only female judge and prophetess. Deborah called Barak to lead warriors into battle against a Canaanite army commander, but Barak would fight only if Deborah went with him.

**Gideon (Judges 6–8)**—God raised him up to lead Israel against the Midianites.

**Abimelech (Judges 9)**—He was Gideon's son. He killed all but one of his brothers and was made king of Shechem. He was killed when a woman dropped part of a millstone on his head.

**Tola (Judges 10:1–2)**—He judged Israel for 23 years.

**Jair (10:3–5)**—He led Israel for 22 years. He was known for having 30 sons who rode 30 donkeys.

**Jephthah (Judges 10:6–12:7)**—He was Gilead's son, and he judged Israel for six years.

**Ibzan (Judges 12:8–10)**—He led the nation for seven years. Ibzan sent his daughters abroad and brought in 30 foreign women as wives for his sons.

**Elon (Judges 12:11–12)**—He judged Israel for 10 years.

**Abdon (Judges 12:13–15)**—He led the nation of Israel for eight years. He was known for having 40 sons and 30 nephews who each rode a donkey.

**Samson (Judges 13–16)**—He was a Nazirite, which meant he had taken a vow not to eat or drink anything from a grapevine, drink alcohol, cut his hair, or eat anything unclean. Samson performed amazing feats of strength, but he had some weaknesses that led to his downfall.

> **WHO, WHAT, WHERE?**
> Gideon was the fifth judge of Israel, and probably the best known of all the judges. God appointed Gideon to lead his nation against the Midianites. The angel of the Lord appeared to Gideon when he was hiding from the enemy, told him God was with him, and called him a "mighty man of valor." Gideon had many doubts, but they did not keep him from obeying God. You can read his story in Judges 6–8.

Samson performed amazing feats of strength.

DISCOVER THE BIBLE

# Ruth

**What It's About:** Ruth was a loyal daughter-in-law of a Hebrew woman named Naomi. After Ruth's husband died, she went on to become an example of faithfulness to God and an object of God's love and care. Ruth and her new husband, Boaz, are the great-grandparents of King David.

**Important Characters/People:** Ruth, Naomi, Boaz

**The Writer:** The writer of the book of Ruth isn't named, but some people believe the prophet Samuel wrote the story.

## What You'll Find in the Book of Ruth

**The story's main** character, Ruth, probably lived around 1100 BC, during the time of the judges.

What makes the book of Ruth different from most other Old Testament books is that Ruth wasn't a Hebrew; she was a native of a place called Moab. She married a Jewish man named Mahlon. Mahlon's mother was a Jewish woman named Naomi. Ruth lived with her husband and his family in Moab.

When Naomi's husband, Elimelech, and her two sons (including Ruth's husband) died, Naomi decided to move back to Bethlehem. Naomi told Ruth and her other daughter-in-law, Orpah, to stay in Moab, but Ruth refused to leave Naomi. The two women traveled to Bethlehem, where Ruth gathered leftover barley during the harvest—a practice called gleaning—so that she and Naomi would have enough food to survive.

As Ruth gathered grain one day, Boaz, the wealthy owner of the field where she was working, noticed her and ordered his workers to protect her and to leave some grain behind for her to collect. When Ruth went home that night, she told Naomi about Boaz, and her mother-in-law recognized him as a relative of Ruth's late husband. Naomi encouraged Ruth to pursue Boaz and make herself available to him.

Boaz was flattered by Ruth's attention, and he eventually married her. Together, they had a son named Obed, who would one day become the grandfather of King David.

### POWER WORDS

*Ruth replied, "Don't ask me to leave you and turn back. Wherever you go, I will go; wherever you live, I will live. Your people will be my people, and your God will be my God."*

Ruth 1:16

### FUN BIBLE TRIVIA

Ruth and Boaz are mentioned in the New Testament as ancestors of Jesus. Matthew 1:5 lists them as the parents of Obed, the grandfather of King David.

CHAPTER 3: HIS STORY. . .AND THEIR STORY

# 1 Samuel

**What It's About:** The 12 tribes of Israel unite under a king. Even though God never wanted His people to live under the rule of a human king, He allows them to set up an earthly kingdom and even chooses the men who would rule over them.

**Important Characters/People:** Hannah, Eli, Samuel, Saul, David, Jonathan, the Philistines, Abigail

**The Writer:** The writer of the book of 1 Samuel isn't named, but some experts believe Samuel himself wrote most of it. Some of the history in this book takes place after Samuel's death, and it is not known who wrote the remainder of the book.

## What You'll Find in the Book of 1 Samuel

This book tells two stories. First, there's the life of the prophet Samuel, who was Israel's last judge (chapters 1–12). Then there is the life of Saul, Israel's first king (chapters 13–31). It starts out with a miracle birth, as a woman named Hannah prays for a son and promises to dedicate him to God's service. God answers by giving her Samuel.

Samuel was one of Israel's greatest prophets. He spoke out against dishonesty in the priesthood and led the people of Israel to turn away from idolatry and back to their God. Samuel spent his entire life as a judge and prophet in Israel.

### This Is Not What God Wanted!

The book of 1 Samuel includes a big change in the nation of Israel. The people ask Samuel for a human king so that they could be just like the other nations around them. Samuel doesn't want Israel to have a king, but he reluctantly prays and tells God what the people want. Even though God warns that having a human king will be disastrous for Israel in the long run, He tells Samuel to appoint a man named Saul as the first king of Israel.

### Who, What, Where?

Eli was a priest during the period of the judges at a place called Shiloh, which was about 10 miles north of Jerusalem. After Hannah's miracle son, Samuel, was weaned, she kept a promise to God and brought him to Eli for service and training. One night, Eli realized God had spoken to Samuel and encouraged the boy to listen and respond. In his first prophecy, Samuel spoke out against the dishonesty of Eli's sons, Hophni and Phinehas, who were both priests.

## DISCOVER THE BIBLE

Saul's reign as king starts out well, but later he makes several bad decisions. Because he disobeys God several times, God removes his blessing from Saul and appoints a young shepherd named David as Israel's second king.

Chapter 16 is the story of Samuel's journey to Bethlehem to anoint David as Israel's next king. Chapter 17 covers David's famous battle with a giant Philistine named Goliath. David's victory over Goliath makes him a hero to everyone in Israel except King Saul, who tries several times to kill David. With God's help, David escapes from Saul several times. (You can read the whole story in chapters 19–26.)

In the final chapter of 1 Samuel, Saul's three sons, including Jonathan (a close friend of David's), die in battle with the Philistines, and Saul commits suicide, clearing the way for David to take the throne of Israel.

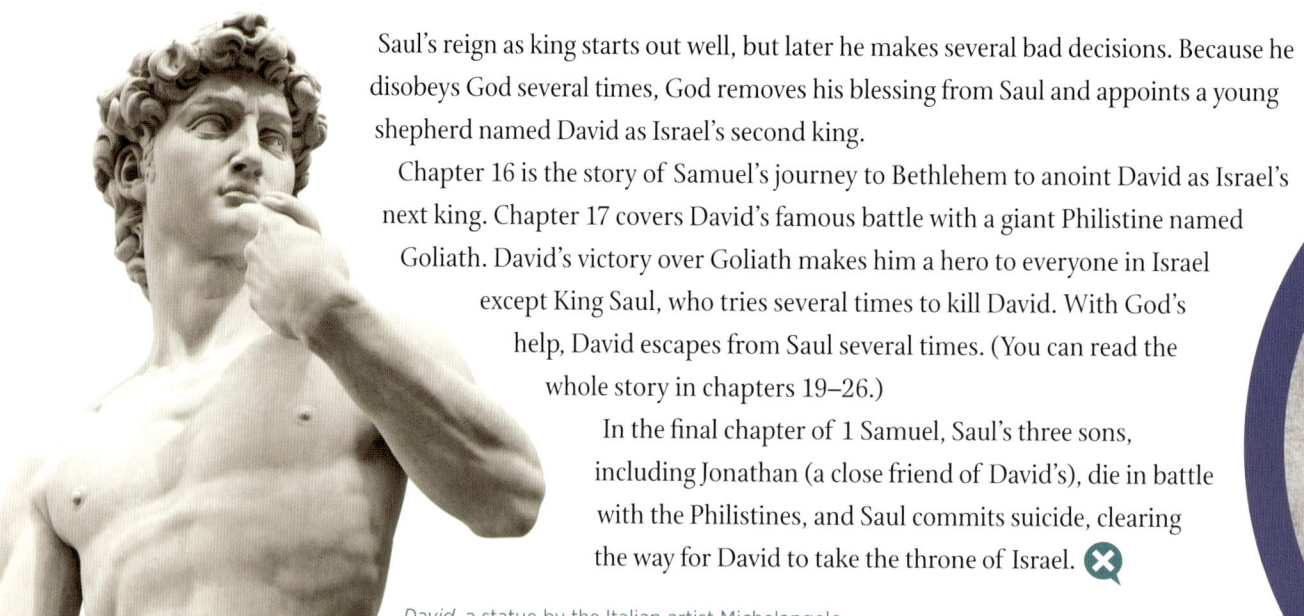

*David*, a statue by the Italian artist Michelangelo, was created between the years 1501 and 1504.

### POWER WORDS

*David replied to the Philistine, "You come to me with sword, spear, and javelin, but I come to you in the name of the L*ORD *of Heaven's Armies—the God of the armies of Israel, whom you have defied."*

1 Samuel 17:45

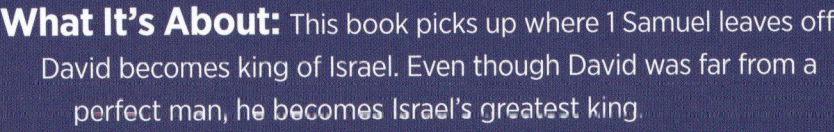

# 2 Samuel

**What It's About:** This book picks up where 1 Samuel leaves off. David becomes king of Israel. Even though David was far from a perfect man, he becomes Israel's greatest king.

**Important Characters/People:** David, Joab, Abner, Ishbosheth, Absalom, Michal, Bathsheba, Uriah, Nathan, Hushai

**The Writer:** Unknown, but it wasn't Samuel, because the events recorded in this book take place after his death. Some suggest that Abiathar the priest was the author (15:35).

## What You'll Find in the Book of 2 Samuel

**Second Samuel covers** about 40 years of Israel's history—the entire reign of David as king of Israel. After King Saul died, David took the throne of the tribe of Judah. Seven years later, after the death of Ishbosheth, the son of Saul and king of the northern tribes, David became king over all Israel.

After capturing Jerusalem from the Jebusites, David made Jerusalem the capital city of Israel. That was the first of many military victories for Israel under King David. After that, Israel became a powerful and rich nation.

One spring, though, David stayed home from battle and committed a terrible sin with Bathsheba, the wife of Uriah, one of his most devoted soldiers. To cover up what he had done, David arranged to have Uriah killed in battle. Even though David repented for his sins and was forgiven, the consequences of what he did affected the rest of his reign—as well as his own family.

David's son Absalom tried to take the throne of Israel from his father. David had to run for his life away from Jerusalem. Eventually, Absalom died in battle, and David returned to Jerusalem to take back the throne. The final three chapters of 2 Samuel tell the story of David's final days.

DISCOVER THE BIBLE

# 1 and 2 Kings

**What They're About:** First Kings starts with the reign of Solomon, David's son, as king of Israel, and 2 Kings ends with both parts of a divided kingdom—the northern kingdom (Israel) and the southern kingdom (Judah)—being defeated and their people taken into captivity. The northern kingdom was defeated by the Assyrians, and the southern kingdom was defeated by the Babylonians.

**Important Characters/People:** David, Adonijah, Solomon, Rehoboam, Jeroboam, Abijam, Asa, Jehoshaphat, Ahab, Jezebel, Nathan, Ahijah, Elijah, and Micaiah in 1 Kings; Elijah, Elisha, Jehoram, Ben-Hadad, Hazael, Ahaziah, Jehu, Jezebel, Ahab, Joash, Ahaz, Isaiah, Hezekiah, Josiah, and Nebuchadnezzar in 2 Kings

**The Writer:** First Kings and 2 Kings were originally one book in the Hebrew Bible. No writer is mentioned, but tradition teaches that the prophet Jeremiah—the same one who wrote the book of Jeremiah—recorded this time in biblical history.

## POWER WORDS

*"Give me an understanding heart so that I can govern your people well and know the difference between right and wrong. For who by himself is able to govern this great people of yours?"*

1 Kings 3:9

# What You'll Find in the Books of 1 and 2 Kings

**First Kings covers** events from around 970 BC to 850 BC. It begins with the last days of King David, moves through the reign of King Solomon, and ends with the story of Elijah, a powerful prophet of God.

# CHAPTER 3: HIS STORY. . .AND THEIR STORY

The first 11 chapters of 1 Kings tell the story of the reign of King Solomon, who started his reign as king of Israel very well. He asked for and received wisdom from God, built the Temple in Jerusalem, and ruled over Israel as it reached its high point in power and standing in that part of the world.

Solomon had it all—power, riches, and respect from his neighbors. Sadly, though, he didn't finish his time as king of Israel the way he started it. In fact, he led God's chosen people down a terrible path that would end with a divided nation at war with itself.

## It's All Downhill from Here—Again

**Like his father,** David, Solomon had a weakness for women that would eventually bring him and his nation down. After spending seven years constructing the Temple for God, Solomon spent the next 13 years building a palace for himself. He also married 700 women, many of whom were foreigners who persuaded him to worship their false gods.

After Solomon's death, his son Rehoboam made some big mistakes that led to the division of the nation of Israel. When all was said and done, the 10 northern tribes formed their own nation under Jeroboam, a former official under Solomon. That nation is called Israel. The two southern tribes made up a nation called Judah.

### Who, What, Where?

Both Israel and Judah were led by a series of kings who didn't do what God wanted them to do. There were a few exceptions, though. Three kings of Judah—Asa (1 Kings 15:9–24), Jehoshaphat (1 Kings 22:41–50), and Hezekiah (2 Kings 18–20)—stood out as men who did what pleased God and who encouraged their people to follow Him, too.

# Discover the Bible

## Who, What, Where?

In the middle of the stories of Israel's and Judah's kings, you can read about two powerful prophets who lived during those times. Elijah is remembered for prophesying that no rain would fall on Israel—which it didn't for three years, until he said it would—and for a showdown at Mount Carmel with the prophets of Baal (1 Kings 18:18–40). Elisha started out as Elijah's student, and he continued the work Elijah had done after Elijah was taken up to heaven in a whirlwind (2 Kings 2:1–15). Both men performed many amazing miracles.

Starting in 1 Kings 12, you can read about the kings (and one queen) of Israel and Judah. Each nation was ruled over by about 20 kings during that time. For the most part, it's not a very positive story. None of the kings of Israel followed God, and only a few of Judah's kings were godly men. They took part in idol worship and encouraged their people to do the same.

Even though God's prophets warned these kings and the people to turn back to God, both countries strayed further and further from Him as time went on. Eventually, God sent judgment in the form of outside invaders, who brought death, destruction, and slavery.

Second Kings ends with the nation of Israel falling to the Assyrians (chapters 16 and 17) in around 722 BC, and Judah falling to the Babylonians (chapters 24 and 25) in about 585 BC.

Second Kings chapter 25 tells how the armies of Babylonian king Nebuchadnezzar surrounded Jerusalem and then destroyed the city and the Temple and took everything of value from the Temple and the king's palace. The Babylonians also captured thousands of captives and took them away to Babylon, where they stayed for several decades in what is called the Babylonian Captivity.

This "ball and chain" was put on a prisoner's ankle to keep him from trying to run away. The Babylonians probably didn't use balls and chains—but they sure took a lot of prisoners from Jerusalem.

CHAPTER 3: HIS STORY. . .AND THEIR STORY

# 1 and 2 Chronicles

**What They're About:** These books cover much of the same history you read about in 1 and 2 Samuel and 1 and 2 Kings, but with more emphasis on the spiritual side of the stories you read in those other books. The books of Chronicles were written after the Babylonian Captivity to give the people returning to Israel an understanding of how to worship God.

**Important Characters/People:** Saul, David, Nathan, Gad, Solomon, Joab, Jashobeam, and Eleazar in 1 Chronicles; Solomon, Rehoboam, Jeroboam, Abijah, Asa, Jehoshaphat, Ahab, Jehoram, Ahaziah, Joash, Amaziah, Uzziah, Jotham, Ahaz, Hezekiah, Manasseh, Josiah, and Jehoahaz in 2 Chronicles

**The Writer:** Like most of the books of the Old Testament, 1 and 2 Chronicles don't name their writers, but centuries of tradition hold that Ezra the priest wrote them.

# What You'll Find in the Books of 1 and 2 Chronicles

**First Chronicles is** a detailed picture of King David's reign over the nation of Israel. It starts with a nine-chapter family history of King David, starting as far back as Adam and his family. Starting with chapter 10, it picks up with David taking the throne of Israel. It ends with Solomon, David's son, taking the throne after his father's death.

### DID YOU KNOW. . .?

The books titled 1 Chronicles and 2 Chronicles in our Bibles today were originally written as one really long book with a title that meant "the words of the days." The book was divided in two in the third century BC, when the Hebrew Bible (also known as the Old Testament) was translated into Greek.

We often think of "worship" as a music style. But for the people of Israel, it was a whole way of life.

49

## DISCOVER THE BIBLE

### POWER WORDS

He [Solomon] prayed, "O LORD, God of Israel, there is no God like you in all of heaven and earth. You keep your covenant and show unfailing love to all who walk before you in wholehearted devotion."

2 Chronicles 6:14

Second Chronicles covers more than 400 years of history. It begins with the construction of Solomon's Temple and ends with Cyrus's announcement that the Jews would be allowed to rebuild the Temple following the Babylonian Captivity. This book focuses mostly on the southern kingdom of Judah and barely mentions the northern kingdom of Israel. It mentions the invasion of Judah by the Babylonians, but focuses more on the good things that happened there.

# Ezra

**What It's About:** After about 70 years of captivity in Babylon, the Jews return to Israel, where for a time they live lives of obedience and devotion to God.

**Important Characters/People:** Darius, Cyrus, Artaxerxes, Ezra, Zerubbabel, Zechariah, Haggai

**The Writer:** The book of Ezra doesn't name its writer, but thousands of years of tradition hold that Ezra himself wrote it. Ezra's name first appears in the book in chapter 7—the same time that the writer changes from writing in the third person to the first person (from "he" to "I").

CHAPTER 3: HIS STORY. . .AND THEIR STORY

# What You'll Find in the Book of Ezra

**This book covers** about one hundred years of history, starting in about 530 BC. The book of Ezra begins where the book of 2 Chronicles ends. King Cyrus of Persia declares that the captive Jews will be allowed to return to their homeland, where they will rebuild the Temple, which had been destroyed when the Babylonians raided Jerusalem seven decades earlier.

The first six chapters of the book of Ezra tell the story of how a first group of Jews, led by a man named Zerubbabel, left Persia and traveled home to Jerusalem to build the second Temple. In between chapters 6 and 7 is a gap of about 58 years, and chapters 7–10 cover the ministry of Ezra, a priest who was accompanied by Israel's religious leaders.

Zerubbabel led a group of people who would build the new Temple. Ezra led a group who reestablished what the Temple stood for in Jerusalem: a growing relationship with God.

### Who, What, Where?

Cyrus was the king of Persia who commanded that the Jewish people be released from captivity so they could return to their home country. He also ordered his people to give donations to help the Jews and returned the Temple vessels that Nebuchadnezzar of Babylon had taken when he took the people of Judah into captivity.

### What's in it for Me?

The story told in the book of Ezra shows just how willing God is to offer His people second chances. God had punished the people of Judah for their disobedience, but now He is giving them a fresh start in their homeland. Here's the really cool thing you need to remember: the same God who gave those wayward people a second chance is more than willing to do the same thing for you after you've made a bad decision.

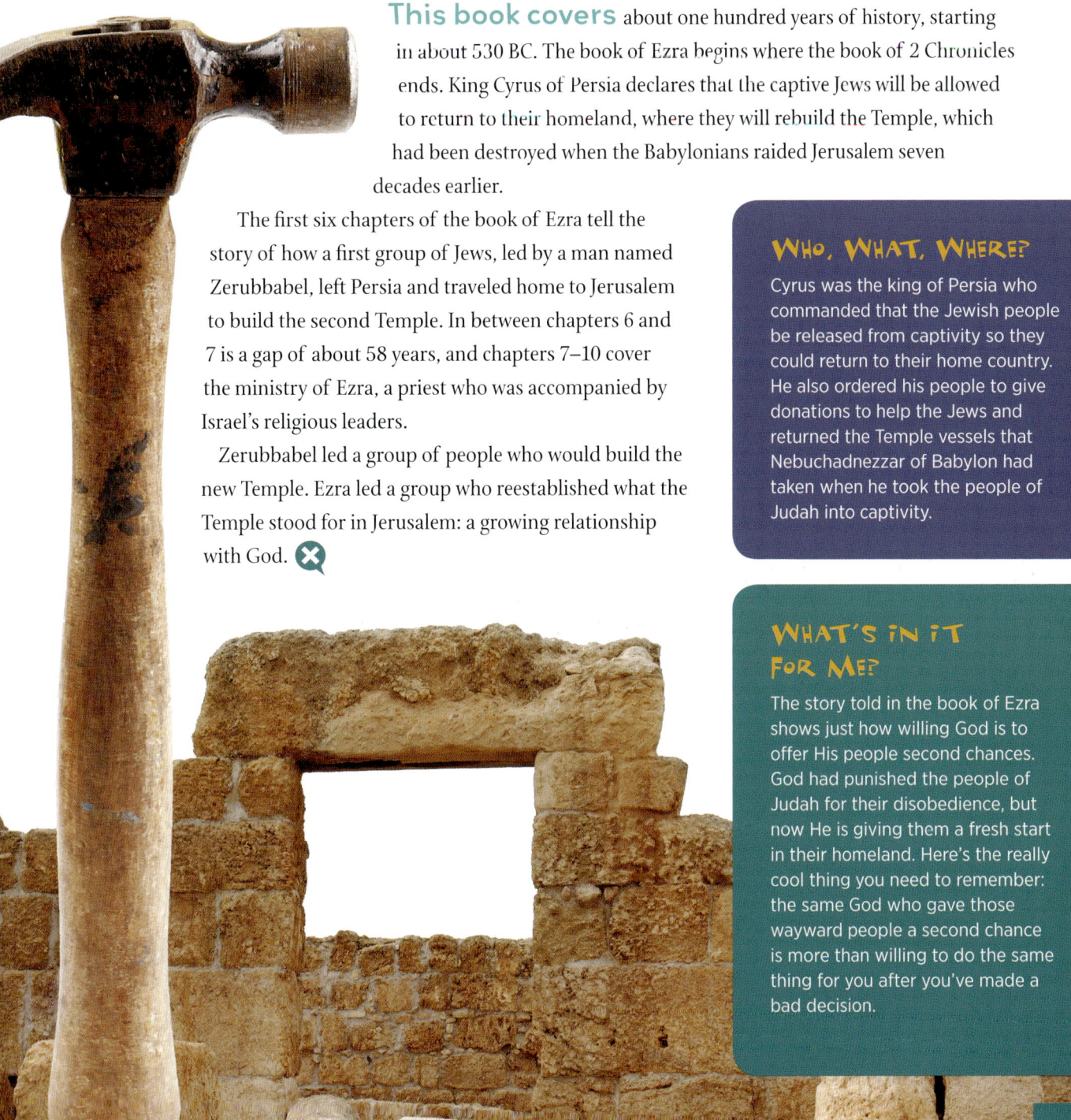

DISCOVER THE BIBLE

# Nehemiah

**What It's About:** The Jewish people, who have just returned to Israel from Babylon, rebuild the walls of the city of Jerusalem.

**Important Characters/People:** Nehemiah, Artaxerxes, Sanballat, Tobiah, Geshem

**The Writer:** This book starts out, "The words of Nehemiah" (1:1 NKJV), but according to Jewish tradition, Ezra wrote the book of Nehemiah.

### Power Words

*"Go and enjoy choice food and sweet drinks, and send some to those who have nothing prepared. This day is sacred to our Lord. Do not grieve, for the joy of the Lord is your strength."*

Nehemiah 8:10 NIV

### Who, What, Where?

Nehemiah and the rest of the Jews received plenty of opposition as they worked to rebuild Jerusalem's walls. Three guys, named Sanballat, Tobiah, and Geshem, plotted to attack Jerusalem, which forced the Jews to guard the uncompleted walls. Tobiah and Sanballat hired a man to warn Nehemiah that he would be killed, and Tobiah sent threatening letters to scare Nehemiah.

## What You'll Find in the Book of Nehemiah

**Nehemiah lived around** the same time as Ezra and led the third and final group of Jews from Persia back to their homeland of Judah. He served as Persian King Artexerxes's cupbearer—the man whose job it was to taste the king's food and wine to make sure someone hadn't put poison in them. The king liked Nehemiah, and when Nehemiah heard that the walls around the city of Jerusalem hadn't been rebuilt, Artaxerxes gave him permission to return to Jerusalem.

The Temple had been rebuilt, but there were no walls around the city to protect it from its many enemies. Nehemiah wanted to go to Jerusalem and encourage the people to get busy rebuilding the city walls.

CHAPTER 3: HIS STORY. . .AND THEIR STORY

The book of Nehemiah tells us how he led a team of builders from Persia to Jerusalem to rebuild the city's walls. With Nehemiah cheering them on—and giving them a little push from behind—the people gave money, supplies, and manpower toward rebuilding the walls. Even though Israel's enemies didn't want the walls rebuilt, the work was completed in just 52 days—a feat that even Israel's enemies saw was the result of God's power.

Not long after the walls were finished, Ezra the priest read the Law of Moses to the people out loud "from early morning until noon" (8:3). That was just the beginning of a spiritual renewal among the people of Israel. Nehemiah also helped reestablish true worship through prayer and encouraged the people to read and obey the Word of God.

# Esther

**What It's About:** Esther, a beautiful Jewish girl who becomes queen of Persia through her marriage to King Ahasuerus (also known as Xerxes), helps save her people from slaughter.

**Important Characters/People:** Xerxes, Mordecai, Haman, Esther, Hathach

**The Writer:** The book of Esther doesn't name its author, but one of the most popular traditions is that Mordecai, Esther's cousin, wrote it. Some believe that Ezra or Nehemiah wrote this book.

# What You'll Find in the Book of Esther

**The story of** Esther takes place during the 58-year gap in the book of Ezra (the one between chapters 6 and 7). Many of the Jews who had been held captive all their lives in Persia wanted to stay there. It was, after all, the only place they'd ever known as home.

53

# DISCOVER THE BIBLE

### FUN BIBLE TRIVIA

It might surprise you to know this, but the name of God doesn't appear anywhere in the book of Esther. In fact, there are no mentions of service to God of any kind in this book. Yet this story shows the hand of God at work in saving His people from what looked like certain death at the hands of the Persians.

The book of Esther tells the story of how Esther becomes queen of Persia then finds herself and her people threatened by a plot to kill all the Jews in Persia. Esther knew that speaking up to her husband, the king, was dangerous, but she was willing to risk her own life to save the lives of the Jews still living in Persia.

Esther's courage to save God's chosen people is celebrated in the annual Jewish festival of Purim, which is still celebrated today.

# CHAPTER 4

# Words to Live By

God's Written Wisdom (Job through Song of Solomon)

**So far, we've** covered books with a lot of history—how things began and what happened after they got their start. Now we're moving on to five books that are often called the Bible's *wisdom literature*.

You can learn a lot about how God wants you to live by reading just about any part of the Bible, but these books are devoted to teaching wisdom for life. In these books are simple instructions for how to maintain your relationship to God, how to get along with other people, and how to be the kind of person God wants you to be.

Out of all the wisdom books, only one—Job—tells someone's story. The rest are mostly collections of thoughts on certain subjects. . .and about God Himself.

## Job

**What It's About:** Job was a good man who loved God but who went through a terrible time of suffering after God allowed Satan to take everything Job had, including his family, his wealth, and his health.

**Important Characters/People:** Job, God, Satan, Eliphaz, Bildad, Zophar, Elihu

**The Writer:** Many experts believe that Job is the oldest book in the Bible—even older than Genesis. Jewish tradition says that Moses wrote the book of Job, but the writer isn't known for certain.

DISCOVER THE BIBLE

### Who, What, Where?

Uz was a land east of Judah. Uz was the name of the son of Aram and grandson of Shem (Genesis 10:23; 1 Chronicles 1:17), and many experts believe the land where Job lived was named after him. In Jeremiah's prophecies, Uz is listed among the lands on which God's anger would fall through the conquest of the Chaldean king Nebuchadnezzar.

### Power Words

"I came naked from my mother's womb, and I will be naked when I leave. The Lord gave me what I had, and the Lord has taken it away. Praise the name of the Lord!"
Job 1:21

# What You'll Find in the Book of Job

**The story of** Job takes place during the time of the patriarchs (Abraham, Isaac, Jacob, and Joseph). Job lived with his family—his wife and seven sons and three daughters—in a place called Uz, and he had everything going for him. He owned 7,000 sheep, 3,000 camels, 500 teams of oxen, and 500 female donkeys. In those days, a person's wealth was measured by how many animals he owned, so it's no wonder the Bible calls Job the wealthiest man living in Uz.

But Job's riches aren't the first thing the Bible tells us about him. The very first verse in the book of Job says, "He was honest inside and out, a man of his word, who was totally devoted to God and hated evil with a passion" (Job 1:1 MSG).

Job was such a great example of godliness and character that God bragged on him a little bit when He said to Satan, "He is the finest man in all the earth. He is blameless—a man of complete integrity. He fears God and stays away from evil" (Job 1:8).

Job sounds like just the kind of guy God would protect from suffering and loss, doesn't he? But if you know anything at all about the book of Job, you know that Job went through a time of terrible suffering and loss.

The devil wasn't impressed with what God had to say about Job, and he challenged God to allow him to take away from Job everything he had—his family, his livestock, and his health. When that happened, the devil said, Job would curse God to His face.

God told Satan he could do what he wanted with Job, but with one limit: the devil wasn't allowed to take Job's life.

# CHAPTER 4: WORDS TO LIVE BY

What followed for Job was suffering on a level that most of us would find hard to imagine. Not only did Job lose his children and his wealth, but he was also covered from head to toe in painful sores called boils. To make matters worse, Job's wife provided no comfort, and when his three best friends came to Uz to "comfort" him, they spent most of their time accusing him of committing some terrible sin against God that led to his suffering.

Most of the book of Job (chapters 3–37) is an account of conversations between Job and his friends—Eliphaz, Bildad, and Zophar—as they try to make sense out of something that made no earthly sense: a good man's horrible suffering, even when he hadn't done anything wrong.

Job cannot understand why all this has happened to him, and finally he calls on God to help him understand. Chapters 38–41 are an account of another conversation—between Job and God.

God confronts Job with question after question about His own character and power. Job has no answer for any of them. In the end, Job realizes that even when he can't make sense of his suffering, he must still remain loyal to the God who had blessed him with so much and then allowed it to be taken away.

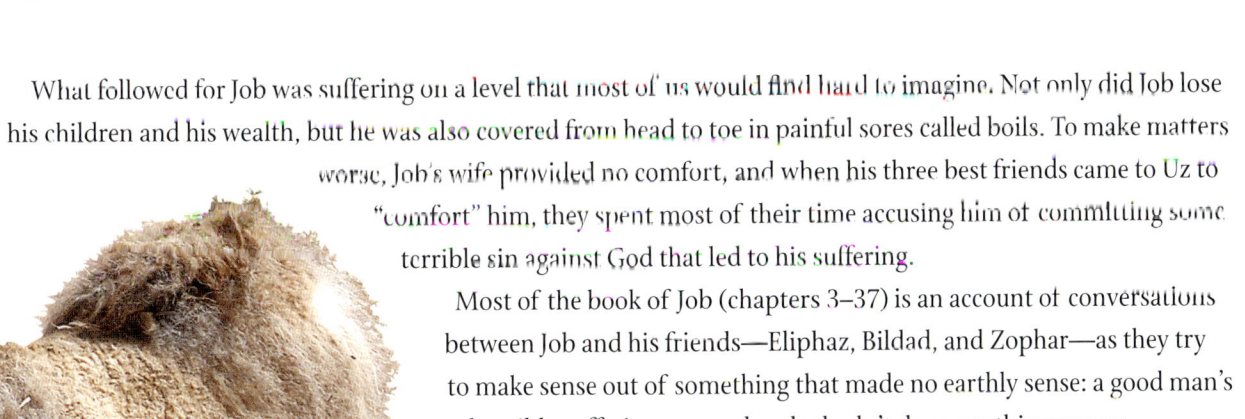

## WHAT'S IN IT FOR ME?

Have you ever gone through a tough time when you wondered if you had done something to deserve it? One of the lessons from the book of Job is that bad things *do* happen to good people, even when they haven't done anything wrong. But don't worry—the Bible promises that God will use everything that happens to you for your own good and for His benefit (see Romans 8:28).

DISCOVER THE BIBLE

# Psalms

**What It's About:** The book of Psalms is actually a collection of songs, poems, and other writings that showcase the different writers' praise, prayers—and complaints—to God as well as their thoughts *about* God.

**Important Characters/People:** David, Asaph, Solomon, the sons of Korah, Moses, Heman, Ethan

**The Writers:** At least seven different writers contributed to the book of Psalms. Of those, King David is credited with the most—at least 73. Other notable psalmists (people who wrote psalms) include Solomon, Moses (yes, the same Moses who led the people of Israel out of Egypt), Asaph, Ethan, and the sons of Korah. Forty-eight of the 150 psalms are not attributed to a specific writer.

## What You'll Find in the Book of Psalms

The book of Psalms includes writings by people who were going through some of the same things you will experience at different times in your life—happiness, sadness, anger, pain, fear, and other strong feelings. Sometimes it's good to read the psalms so you can understand that you're not alone, that other people have felt the same feelings you might be feeling right now.

### FUN BIBLE TRIVIA

If you were to take your Bible in your hand and try to open it so that you were in the very middle, you'd probably see one of the psalms. The middle chapter of the Bible is Psalm 117 and the middle verse is Psalm 118:8.

The Bible includes 150 psalms. The book of Psalms is by far the longest book in the Bible. It also includes the shortest chapter in the Bible (Psalm 117) and the longest chapter (Psalm 119).

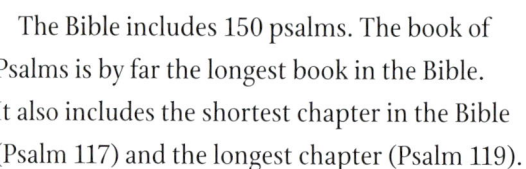

## CHAPTER 4: WORDS TO LIVE BY

The word *psalm* comes from a Greek word that means "a song sung to the accompaniment of a plucked (or string) instrument." The Jewish people used the psalms as Temple hymns during their worship services.

The book of Psalms, which is also called the Psalter, was written over a long time period: from about 1100 BC to around 430 BC. Psalm 90, which was written by Moses, is clearly the oldest of the psalms.

Because the psalms were written as poetry, they use a lot of word pictures to describe what God is like. Here are just a few of the many, many ways God is presented in the psalms:

Creator (8:3–4)
Deliverer (18:2)
Father (68:5–6)
King (93:1–2)
Refuge (46:1)
Shepherd (23:1)
Shield (3:3)
Teacher (25:8–9)
Warrior (35:1–3)

While the psalms describe the many parts of God's character, they also put into words people's feelings about Him. In the psalms, you'll find words of praise for God, confessions of sin to God, expressions of confidence in God. You'll even find words of disappointment and frustration with God from people who were going through difficult times and wondered if God was really there for them. (Hint: The psalmists usually came around to the

### WHO, WHAT, WHERE?

The Asaph who wrote Psalms 50 and 73–83 was a descendant of Abraham through Jacob's son Levi. He was one of the key musicians serving in the Jerusalem Temple during the time of King David. David appointed Asaph's descendants "to proclaim God's messages to the accompaniment of lyres, harps, and cymbals" (1 Chronicles 25:1).

### POWER WORDS

*The LORD is my shepherd; I have all that I need. He lets me rest in green meadows; he leads me beside peaceful streams. He renews my strength. He guides me along right paths, bringing honor to his name.*

Psalm 23:1–3

### DID YOU KNOW...?

The book of Psalms is divided into five smaller collections, based on the time periods in which historians believe they were written or compiled. The five books are as follows:

Book One (Psalms 1–41): Psalms compiled, and mostly written, by David.
Book Two (Psalms 42–72): Psalms written by the sons of Korah and by David; likely compiled while Hezekiah was king of Judah.
Book Three (Psalms 73–89): Psalms written during the reigns of kings Hezekiah and Manasseh, but compiled while King Josiah ruled.
Book Four (Psalms 90–106): Includes the rest of the psalms written prior to the Babylonian Captivity, including one by Moses and a couple by David; the rest are by unknown writers.
Book Five (Psalms 107–150): Psalms written during the Jews' return from the Babylonian Captivity. Books four and five may have been compiled during the time of the prophet Nehemiah.

## DISCOVER THE BIBLE

### WHAT'S IN IT FOR ME?

The very middle verse of the Bible—meaning there are the same number of verses before it and after it—is Psalm 118:8, which says, "It is better to trust in the LORD than to put confidence in man" (NKJV). If God placed that verse in the center of the Bible, what does it tell you about what you should put at the center of your life?

conclusion that God really was there, even when it seemed He was millions of miles away!) Many of the psalms ask God some really tough questions!

# Proverbs

**What It's About:** This book is mostly a collection of short sayings and thoughts to encourage people of different ages and life situations to follow God and seek out wisdom. The book of Proverbs is different from most other books of the Bible in that it doesn't have a story line, but is instead a collection of practical tips for wise and godly living.

**Important Characters/People:** Solomon, Agur, Lemuel

**The Writers:** Most experts agree that the first 29 chapters of the book of Proverbs were written by a man known for his wisdom: King Solomon, the third king of Israel and son of King David. Solomon wrote his proverbs during his reign as king of Israel, which began around 1015 to 1020 BC. Chapter 30 of the book of Proverbs is credited to someone named Agur, who may have been a friend of Solomon's or who may have been Solomon himself, writing under another name. Chapter 31 is credited to King Lemuel. It is suggested by some that Lemuel is the name Bathsheba, Solomon's mother, gave to Solomon, so this may be a proverb from Bathsheba.

CHAPTER 4: WORDS TO LIVE BY

# What You'll Find in the Book of Proverbs

**Solomon's purpose for** writing the proverbs—as well as the rewards for living by them—is found early in the book, in Proverbs 1:2–6. Solomon writes that he intends for these proverbs to give wisdom, instruction, and understanding to the reader, to teach his readers to live carefully.

> **POWER WORDS**
>
> *Trust in the L<small>ORD</small> with all your heart; do not depend on your own understanding. Seek his will in all you do, and he will show you which path to take.*
>
> Proverbs 3:5-6

God told Solomon that He had given the young king wisdom and understanding (1 Kings 3:12). Later in his life, Solomon didn't apply the wisdom God had given him, and it cost him and his kingdom dearly. But he recorded a lot of wisdom in this book and in the next book of the Bible, Ecclesiastes.

Solomon writes that he intends for these proverbs to give wisdom, instruction, and understanding to the reader, to teach his readers to live carefully.

# DISCOVER THE BIBLE

## WHAT'S IN IT FOR ME?

Many times in the book of Proverbs, Solomon calls his readers "my son." In the Hebrew culture of that time, all male descendants of a king were considered that king's sons, so Solomon wrote to give future kings of Israel wisdom and understanding. The book of Proverbs is still a great source of teaching for all young people. Read the book through once and see what kind of wisdom God might be trying to teach you.

During most of Solomon's reign, the nation of Israel was at an all-time high in a lot of areas. The people worshipped God and lived in a time of prosperity. The surrounding nations treated Israel and its king with amazing respect. Leaders from all over the known world traveled to Israel to hear Solomon speak (see 1 Kings 4:34).

Chapter 31 begins by discouraging the use of strong drink, and continues by describing the perfect wife.

Sometimes, the proverbs included together in the same chapter seem completely unrelated to one another, but they all speak to important life issues, such as work, money, relationships, temptation, drinking, laziness, discipline, seeking God, and raising children.

CHAPTER 4: WORDS TO LIVE BY

# Ecclesiastes

**What It's About:** "These are the words of the Teacher, King David's son, who ruled in Jerusalem" (1:1). The book of Ecclesiastes points out that life is futile and meaningless when we don't seek and follow God as our top priority.

**Important Characters/People:** The Teacher, God, wise men, fools

**The Writer:** The book of Ecclesiastes doesn't name its author, but several verses imply that it was King Solomon. Some experts believe Solomon wrote this book late in his life to help teach others the lessons he had learned from his own wrong choices.

## What You'll Find in the Book of Ecclesiastes

**Early in his** reign as king of Israel, Solomon followed his father's instructions to the letter. He followed God and kept all His commandments. God rewarded Solomon's faithfulness by giving him power, prosperity, popularity, and other earthly blessings. Sadly, later in his life, Solomon abandoned his God and chased after worldly pleasures he had been warned about. The results were disastrous—for Solomon himself and for the kingdom of Israel.

Solomon reigned as king from around 970 BC to about 930 BC. Bible experts believe he wrote the book of Ecclesiastes near the end of his reign—around 935 BC. If Solomon is the author of this book, then it is the reflections of a man who had learned some very hard lessons. He had every earthly blessing a man could want—money, power, respect, just to

### POWER WORDS

*Don't let the excitement of youth cause you to forget your Creator. Honor him in your youth before you grow old and say, "Life is not pleasant anymore."*

Ecclesiastes 12:1

### WHAT'S IN IT FOR ME?

Solomon wrote, "Whatever you do, do well" (Ecclesiastes 9:10). That's great advice. Ask yourself, do you do everything you do to the best of your ability? Are you the best son or daughter you can be? The best brother or sister you can be? Are you the best student you can be?

63

## DISCOVER THE BIBLE

### WHAT'S IN IT FOR ME?

In the end, after writing about a life of futility and hopelessness apart from God, the Teacher in the book of Ecclesiastes concludes with these wise words: "Fear God and keep His commandments, for this is man's all. For God will bring every work into judgment, including every secret thing, whether good or evil" (12:13–14 NKJV). That's great advice for anyone to follow!

name a few—but he understood that none of those things was enough to give him a life of joy and happiness. True fulfillment came only when he made God the center of everything he did.

Throughout Ecclesiastes, the word *vanity* (other translations use the word *meaningless*) and the phrase "under the sun" occur repeatedly. The lesson of this book is that everything we can enjoy in this world (under the sun) will one day be left behind; and it all means nothing if we don't make God the center of everything we do, say, and think.

The first seven chapters of this book are the words of a very unhappy man. He has tried to find fulfillment in knowledge, worldly wisdom, riches, work, and other things. But he realizes these things, though they may bring some pleasure for a while, won't give him the purpose, fulfillment, and happiness that can be found only in eternal things.

The final four chapters of Ecclesiastes are the Teacher's advice on how we should live if we want to find purpose, fulfillment, and happiness. He has left God and tried everything else "under the sun" and has learned (the hard way) that the very best this world has to offer is nothing compared with living a life centered on loving God and keeping His commandments. (Read the Teacher's words in chapter 12.)

CHAPTER 4: WORDS TO LIVE BY

# Song of Solomon (also known as Song of Songs)

**What It's About:** Solomon writes about the beauty of married love. Though the name of God is never mentioned in this book, some experts believe the Song of Solomon was written to compare the love of a devoted spouse to the love of God, who is deeply devoted to His people.

**Important Characters/People:** The husband and his wife

**The Writer:** King Solomon wrote more than 1,000 songs, but he calls this his "Song of Songs." Some experts believe it's possible that Solomon didn't write this book but that it was written *about* him.

## What You'll Find in the Song of Solomon

**The two main** characters in this book are Solomon and his wife, the beautiful young Shulamite woman. The words in the poem are those of Solomon, the young woman, and the daughters of Jerusalem.

### POWER WORDS

*He escorts me to the banquet hall; it's obvious how much he loves me.*

Song of Solomon 2:4

# DISCOVER THE BIBLE

In one of the Bible's weirdest visions, the prophet Ezekiel sees dry, long-dead skeletons being covered with muscles and skin, and coming back to life. This painting, from 1630, is an artist's idea of how Ezekiel 37 might have looked.

# CHAPTER 5

## God's Messengers

### Major and Minor Prophets (Isaiah through Malachi)

**The Old Testament** includes 17 "prophetic" books—books that warn people of God's judgment and encourage them with promises of forgiveness and restoration if they will turn back to Him.

The Old Testament includes the writings of five "major" prophets and 12 "minor" prophets. The difference isn't that the minor prophets are less important than the others, but that their books are much shorter than those of Isaiah, Jeremiah (who also wrote Lamentations), Ezekiel, and Daniel.

The books of Old Testament prophecy include some of the best-known stories in the Bible. For example, you can read about Daniel in the lions' den and his friends Shadrach, Meshach, and Abednego in the book of Daniel, and you can read about the prophet Jonah finding himself stuck in a giant fish's belly in the book of Jonah.

## Isaiah

**What It's About:** Even though the people of Israel had fallen away from God and would suffer the consequences of their sin, God promises a Messiah to provide forgiveness and save them from their sins.

**Important Characters/People:** Isaiah, King Hezekiah, the Messiah, kings of Judah and Israel

**The Writer:** The prophet Isaiah was the son of a man named Amoz, and his ministry to the people of Judah began during the reign of King Uzziah and ended during the reign of King Hezekiah. Isaiah preached during the reigns of four kings. The book of Isaiah was written between 701 and 681 BC.

DISCOVER THE BIBLE

# What You'll Find in the Book of Isaiah

**Like the other** Old Testament prophets, Isaiah warned the people that they faced God's punishment for their sin. But He also wrote about the coming Messiah, a Savior who would take the punishment for the people's sins and give them peace with God. In fact, chapters 40–66 of Isaiah's long prophecy describe God's restoration of Israel, His promised salvation, and His eternal kingdom.

### POWER WORDS

*He was pierced for our rebellion, crushed for our sins. He was beaten so we could be whole. He was whipped so we could be healed. All of us, like sheep, have strayed away. We have left God's paths to follow our own. Yet the L*ORD *laid on him the sins of us all.*

Isaiah 53:5–6

The prophet Isaiah preached mostly to the kingdom of Judah. At that time, Judah's relationship with God was up and down. There were times when the people stuck close to God, but there were also times when they rebelled against Him.

One interesting fact about the book of Isaiah: it is the Old Testament prophetic book most often quoted in the New Testament (the Psalms are the most quoted book overall). The New Testament directly quotes Isaiah 66 times. Also, Isaiah contains more prophecies about Jesus than any other Old Testament book of prophecy.

The book of Isaiah contains literally dozens of prophecies about the life and work of Jesus. These include His virgin birth (7:14), that His ministry would include healing people of sickness and disease (35:5–6), and that He would suffer and die willingly to give people forgiveness and peace with God (53).

### WHAT'S IN IT FOR ME?

Look up Isaiah 9:1–2 and you'll find a wonderful promise that the Jewish Messiah—Jesus—would come not only for the Jews but for all people. That means that no matter what race or people group you come from, Jesus came to earth and lived, died, and was raised from the dead for you!

Isaiah contains more prophecies about Jesus than any other Old Testament book of prophecy.

CHAPTER 5: GOD'S MESSENGERS

# Jeremiah

**What It's About:** The prophet Jeremiah warns the people of Judah of coming punishment and suffering because they have abandoned God.

**Important Characters/People:** Jeremiah, King Jehoiakim, Hananiah, Baruch

**The Writer:** Jeremiah was a young boy when God called him to be a prophet (1:6). He was the son of a priest named Hilkiah. His ministry started during the reign of King Josiah (about 617 BC) and ended several years after the Babylonians destroyed Jerusalem, an event he foretold in his writings.

## What You'll Find in the Book of Jeremiah

**Jeremiah's message to** the people of Judah was pretty much all bad news. God had given the people warning after warning through earlier prophets to turn back to Him, but they had refused. Jeremiah warned that God would send the Babylonians to destroy Jerusalem and take the people of Judah into captivity.

The people of Judah—especially the leaders—didn't like what Jeremiah had to say. They made fun of Jeremiah, beat him, and imprisoned him. But Jeremiah's words came true. Chapter 52 of his prophetic book describes the Babylonian invasion of Judah.

### POWER WORDS

"O Israel, can I not do to you as this potter has done to his clay? As the clay is in the potter's hand, so are you in my hand."

Jeremiah 18:6

### WHO, WHAT, WHERE?

Baruch was an assistant to Jeremiah who wrote down all the words the prophet received from God and then went to the Temple and read those prophecies to the people. When Baruch read the prophecies to the princes of the land, the princes warned him and Jeremiah to hide. After Jehoiakim, the king of Judah, destroyed the first copy of the prophecies, Baruch rewrote it from Jeremiah's dictation.

69

DISCOVER THE BIBLE

# Lamentations

**What It's About:** The prophet Jeremiah grieves over the destruction that has come on the city of Jerusalem and the people of Judah—the same destruction he had warned about in the book of Jeremiah.

**Important Characters/People:** Jeremiah, Zedekiah, the Babylonians

**The Writer:** Jeremiah the prophet

## What You'll Find in the Book of Lamentations

Jeremiah has often been called "the weeping prophet," and the book of Lamentations shows why. It isn't very pleasant to read the words of a godly man who saw the death and destruction in his homeland and mourns over what has happened.

# Ezekiel

**What It's About:** Even though things look hopeless for the people of Judah, who are living in captivity in Babylon, God promises that their nation will one day be restored.

**Important Characters/People:** Ezekiel, Pelatiah, Jaazaniah, Nebuchadnezzar, Pharaoh

**The Writer:** Ezekiel was a priest and the son of Buzi. He was about 25 years old when he was among the people of Judah who were taken to Babylon after King Nebuchadnezzar attacked Judah and took many of the people of Jerusalem away. About five years later, while Ezekiel was in Babylon, God came to him in a vision and called him to minister to the rebellious Israelites. The book of Ezekiel was probably written between 593 and 565 BC.

# CHAPTER 5: GOD'S MESSENGERS

## What You'll Find in the Book of Ezekiel

**Like Jeremiah, Ezekiel** wrote a lot about God's judgment. But he also wrote about God's love and mercy for His people. Yes, God had judged and punished the people of Judah, but He would also forgive them and one day would allow them to return to their homeland.

The book of Ezekiel can be split into four sections. Chapters 1–24 are about the ruin of Jerusalem when the Babylonians attacked, and chapters 25–32 are about God's judgment on the nations around Jerusalem. In chapter 33, Ezekiel records God's call for His people to turn back to him. Chapters 34–48 are chapters of hope for the nation of Israel, because they promise that Israel will be restored and rebuilt in the future.

> **FUN BIBLE TRIVIA**
> The book of Ezekiel includes the story of the fall of Lucifer (also known as the devil), one of the most beautiful and gifted angels God created. Lucifer was kicked out of heaven long ago because of his pride and because he wanted to be like God Himself.

## Daniel

**What It's About:** Daniel—as well as some of his friends—remain true to God while in captivity in Babylon. God blesses their faithfulness, even though they are in a really tough situation.

**Important Characters/People:** Daniel, Nebuchadnezzar, Darius, Belshazzar, Shadrach, Meshach, Abednego

**The Writer:** Daniel was a young man when the Babylonians destroyed Jerusalem and took many of the people of Judah captive. During the 70-year Babylonian Captivity, Daniel remained true to God in every way and was rewarded with knowledge, wisdom, and power. The book of Daniel was probably written between 540 and 530 BC.

## What You'll Find in the Book of Daniel

**During the Babylonian** Captivity, the prophet Daniel served in King Nebuchadnezzar's royal court. He also served several rulers who succeeded Nebuchadnezzar. In the book of Daniel, you can read about the prophet's actions and the visions and prophecies he received during this time.

## DISCOVER THE BIBLE

### Who, What, Where?

Chapter 3 of the book of Daniel includes an amazing story about three of Daniel's friends—Hananiah, Mishael, and Azariah (also known as Shadrach, Meshach, and Abednego). These three young men refused to worship a gold statue made by King Nebuchadnezzar and were thrown into a fiery furnace as punishment. But God protected them from harm, and amazingly, not a hair on their heads was burned.

Daniel describes and interprets several dreams in this book, including one dream Nebuchadnezzar had about an image of several metals and clay. (You can read the whole story in Daniel 2.) Daniel revealed the meaning of a second dream to Nebuchadnezzar, predicting his downfall until he worshipped God. (That story is found in chapter 4.)

During the reign of King Belshazzar, Nebuchadnezzar's son, Daniel interpreted the meaning of some mysterious handwriting that appeared on the wall during a banquet. As a result, Belshazzar made Daniel the third highest ruler in the kingdom; but later that night, Belshazzar died.

When Darius took over the kingdom of Babylon, he planned to make Daniel head of the whole kingdom, but other leaders plotted against Daniel. They knew he would never worship anyone but God, and they tricked the king into punishing any person who worshipped anyone but the king. For disobeying this law, Daniel was thrown into the lions' den. But when Daniel came out safely, Darius honored the God who had kept Daniel safe. (You can read the whole story in Daniel 6.)

Daniel's prophecies predicted the coming of several important world figures, including Alexander the Great, Cleopatra, and (most important) Jesus Christ.

Rembrandt's painting *Belshazzar's Feast*

CHAPTER 5: GOD'S MESSENGERS

# Hosea

**What It's About:** God calls a prophet to marry an immoral woman named Gomer. When she runs away from Hosea with another man, God tells Hosea to go after her and try to win her back.

**Important Characters/People:** Hosea, Gomer

**The Writer:** Hosea served the people of Israel around the time of the reigns of kings Uzziah of Judah (around 792–750 BC), Jotham of Judah (750–735 BC), Ahaz of Judah (735–715 BC), Hezekiah of Judah (715–697 BC), and Jeroboam of Israel (793–753 BC).

## What You'll Find in the Book of Hosea

**God called Hosea** to live a very difficult family life. He commanded Hosea to marry Gomer, a woman Hosea no doubt knew wouldn't be faithful to him. Gomer wasn't faithful to Hosea, but he went after her to try to win her back to himself. God used Hosea's family life to show the people how He loved them despite their unfaithfulness to Him and how He was working to bring them back to Him.

# Joel

**What It's About:** Swarms of grasshoppers descend on the nation of Israel, devouring every living plant in their path. The grasshoppers are an example of God's judgment on a sinful people. In the middle of this plague, God promises salvation to those who turn to Him.

**Important Characters/People:** Joel, leaders in Jerusalem and Judah

**The Writer:** Joel, the son of Pethuel (Joel 1:1), was an educated man who knew the words of the earlier prophets. It isn't known for certain when Joel prophesied, but some experts believe it was around the time of the reign of King Joash (835–796 BC). The book of Joel was probably written around that time.

DISCOVER THE BIBLE

# What You'll Find in the Book of Joel

**POWER WORDS**
*"But everyone who calls on the name of the Lord will be saved."*
Joel 2:32

**It isn't certain** whether swarms of grasshoppers actually devoured all of Israel's crops or if they were part of a story God used to make a point. Either way, however, Joel used the example to warn the people of what would happen if they didn't turn back to God. If they didn't turn back, armies from surrounding nations would invade and "devour" the land, just as the grasshoppers had devoured all the plants there. But if the people did turn back to God, He would forgive them and bless them.

# Amos

**What It's About:** God wanted His people to understand that He wanted them to treat people fairly and justly, not just to observe a bunch of religious rules.

**Important Characters/People:** Amos, Jeroboam II, Uzziah, Amaziah

**The Writer:** The prophet Amos was a shepherd and fruit picker from a small village in Judah. He was an uneducated man who ministered during the reigns of King Uzziah of Judah and King Jeroboam II of Israel. This book was probably written around 756 BC.

# What You'll Find in the Book of Amos

**Amos's message was** mostly directed to the nation of Israel. Things were going pretty well in Israel at that time, but the people committed many sins, including idolatry, greed, and mistreatment of poor people. Mostly, the people of Israel ignored Amos's warning of God's judgment for their sins.

The first part of this book includes warnings of judgment on the nations around Israel, and then on the nation of Judah. The second part warns of even worse judgment on Israel. Amos's message is clear: God's judgment is coming soon. The book ends like many other Old Testament books of prophecy—with the promise of better things in the future for some of the people of Israel.

CHAPTER 5: GOD'S MESSENGERS

# Obadiah

**What It's About:** God announces that the city of Edom will be judged for taking part in Jerusalem's destruction.

**Important Characters/People:** Obadiah, Edom's leaders

**The Writer:** The prophet Obadiah. The Bible says nothing about Obadiah's family or personal life. The book of Obadiah was probably written around 845 BC.

## What You'll Find in the Book of Obadiah

Obadiah is the shortest book in the Old Testament—only 21 verses. The prophet Obadiah delivers the message that the nation of Edom will be destroyed because the Edomites celebrated the bad things that had happened to Israel and because they fought against Israel after the Israelites asked for Edom's help against their enemies.

### FUN BIBLE TRIVIA

The name Obadiah means "serving God." The prophet Obadiah is one of 13 men by that name in the Old Testament.

# Jonah

**What It's About:** A prophet runs the other way when God tells him to go to a city called Nineveh to preach. Because of his disobedience, Jonah is swallowed by a giant sea creature and stays in its stomach for three days.

**Important Characters/People:** Jonah, the king of Nineveh, the sailors

**The Writer:** This is Jonah's story, but it is written in the third person ("he" instead of "I"), so another writer probably recorded the words. This book was written around 760 BC.

DISCOVER THE BIBLE

# What You'll Find in the Book of Jonah

**Jonah lived and** preached around the time of King Jeroboam II of Israel. When God called him to travel to Nineveh to preach to the people there, Jonah refused. Being a prophet, Jonah knew that the people of Nineveh would become Israel's mortal enemies. He wasn't about to do anything to help them!

Rather than go to Nineveh, Jonah hightailed it to a port city called Joppa, where he boarded a ship bound for Tarshish—exactly the opposite direction God had told him to go. When a violent storm struck, threatening to sink the ship and kill everyone aboard, Jonah confessed to the sailors that he was running from God, and they threw Jonah overboard.

Jonah was swallowed by a big sea creature, and while inside the animal, he had time to think about his actions—and the fact that he was running from God. When Jonah praised God, the creature vomited him onto dry land. Jonah went to Nineveh, just as God had told him to do, and preached there. Amazingly, the people of Nineveh, led by their king, turned to God, who spared the city.

## Who, What, Where?

Nineveh was a large city located on the eastern bank of the Tigris River. The city was built by a descendant of Noah named Asshur (Genesis 10:11), who also built the cities of Rehoboth and Calah (see Genesis 10:11). During the time of Jonah, Nineveh was the capital of the Assyrian Empire.

## What's in it for Me?

The obvious lesson from the book of Jonah is that it's always the best choice to obey when God tells us to do something. But there's another lesson here, and it's one Jesus taught when He told His followers, "Love your enemies! Pray for those who persecute you!" (Matthew 5:44).

CHAPTER 5: GOD'S MESSENGERS

# Micah

**What It's About:** God announces that Judah (the southern kingdom) and Israel (the northern kingdom) will be judged for worshipping idols instead of God and for their mistreatment and abuse of the poor and needy around them.

**Important Characters/People:** Micah, Jotham, Ahaz, Hezekiah

**The Writer:** The prophet Micah was a native of Moresheth in southern Judah who ministered during the reigns of Kings Jotham, Ahaz, and Hezekiah of Judah (750–686 BC). This book was written around 700 BC.

## What You'll Find in the Book of Micah

**Micah preached against** idolatry and cheating the poor and warned that both Judah and Israel would be destroyed by outside invaders.

Like many other prophets, Micah preached a message of God's judgment but also of God's mercy. God would forgive the sins of His people and would not remain angry with them forever—simply because He loves showing mercy.

> **POWER WORDS**
>
> *O people, the LORD has told you what is good, and this is what he requires of you: to do what is right, to love mercy, and to walk humbly with your God.*
>
> Micah 6:8

# Nahum

**What It's About:** The powerful city of Nineveh, which had repented a century earlier when Jonah preached there, will be destroyed for its evilness.

**Important Characters/People:** Nahum, the king of Nineveh

**The Writer:** The prophet Nahum. Nahum lived in a place called Elkosh. He preached to Judah after Assyria had captured Israel. This book was written between 663 and 612 BC.

77

# What You'll Find in the Book of Nahum

**This book of** prophecy is kind of a sequel (continues a story begun in another book) to the book of Jonah. Even though God had shown mercy on the city after the people repented when they heard Jonah preach, they returned to their old ways. The city was destroyed not long after Nahum preached to the people there.

# Habakkuk

**What It's About:** A prophet questions God—and receives an answer—when he learns that God will allow the evil Chaldeans to destroy the nation of Judah.

**Important Characters/People:** Habakkuk, the leaders of Judah, Jehoahaz

**The Writer:** The prophet Habakkuk. Nothing is known of his personal life or his family. He served during the reign of King Josiah of Judah. This book was written around 600 BC.

## What's in it for Me?

Ever been in a situation where you just wanted to tell God, "It's not fair!" If you haven't, you most likely will at some point. Then you can follow Habakkuk's example: Talk to God about your situation. Tell Him what you think is unfair about it. Then wait. Even if you don't have an answer, even if things seem more unfair than ever, trust God and allow Him to use your situation for your best.

# What You'll Find in the Book of Habakkuk

**Being a prophet** of God, Habakkuk knew what was ahead for his nation. It was only a matter of time before Judah's mortal enemies, the Chaldeans, attacked and destroyed Judah.

Habakkuk understood that God had to punish his people's sinful, idolatrous behavior. What he couldn't understand was why God would use such an evil, godless people to do it.

In time, Habakkuk had his answer. And even though it wasn't the answer he wanted, he still accepted that God knew what He was doing and why He was doing it the way He was.

CHAPTER 5: GOD'S MESSENGERS

# Zephaniah

**What It's About:** God warns of a coming "day of the Lord," when His people will face judgment, but He also promises restoration for the nation of Israel.

**Important Characters/People:** Zephaniah, Josiah, Nebuchadnezzar

**The Writer:** Zephaniah was the son of Cushi and great-grandson of King Hezekiah, the godly king of Judah. He preached in the days of King Josiah of Judah (around 640–610 BC). This book was written during that time.

## What You'll Find in the Book of Zephaniah

**Like Jeremiah, Zephaniah** preached of a terrible time of judgment and suffering by the people of Judah because they had moved so far away from their God. Also like Jeremiah, Zephaniah pleaded with the people to seek God before it was too late (Zephaniah 2:1–3).

Zephaniah's book closes with a promising message. Though the prophet agreed that hard times were ahead for his people, he also delivered a message of salvation and restoration (3:8–20).

> **POWER WORDS**
>
> *"For the LORD your God is living among you. He is a mighty savior. He will take delight in you with gladness. With his love, he will calm all your fears. He will rejoice over you with joyful songs."*
>
> Zephaniah 3:17

# Haggai

**What It's About:** The Jews return to Jerusalem after being held captive in Babylon and are commanded to rebuild God's Temple.

**Important Characters/People:** Haggai, Joshua, Darius, Cyrus, Zerubbabel, Shealtiel

**The Writer:** The prophet Haggai preached after the Jews had returned from captivity in Babylon to their homeland. The Bible says nothing about his personal life or his family. This book was written in 520 BC, in the second year of Darius the king (1:1).

DISCOVER THE BIBLE

# What You'll Find in the Book of Haggai

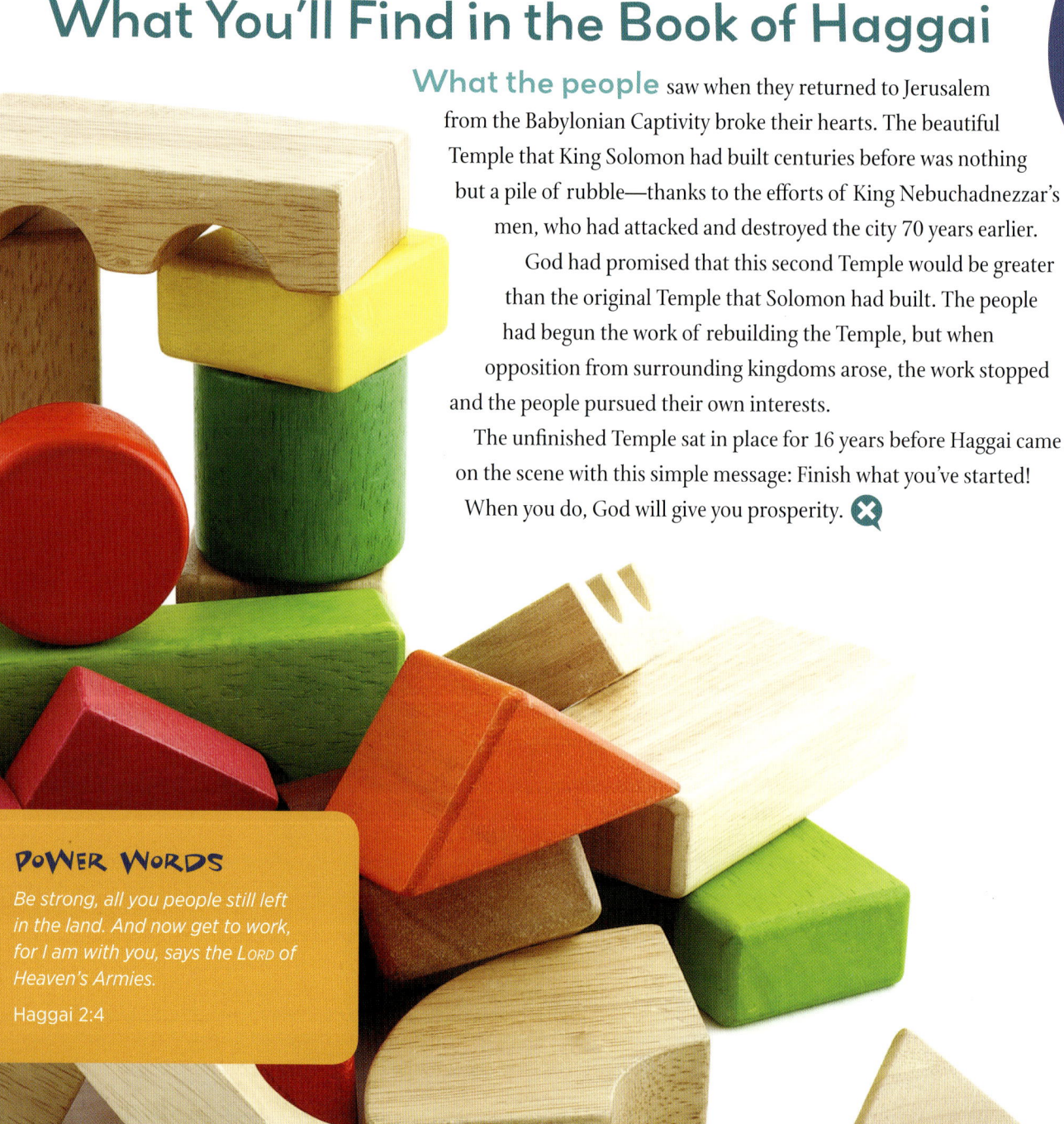

**What the people** saw when they returned to Jerusalem from the Babylonian Captivity broke their hearts. The beautiful Temple that King Solomon had built centuries before was nothing but a pile of rubble—thanks to the efforts of King Nebuchadnezzar's men, who had attacked and destroyed the city 70 years earlier.

God had promised that this second Temple would be greater than the original Temple that Solomon had built. The people had begun the work of rebuilding the Temple, but when opposition from surrounding kingdoms arose, the work stopped and the people pursued their own interests.

The unfinished Temple sat in place for 16 years before Haggai came on the scene with this simple message: Finish what you've started! When you do, God will give you prosperity.

### POWER WORDS

*Be strong, all you people still left in the land. And now get to work, for I am with you, says the L*ORD *of Heaven's Armies.*

Haggai 2:4

CHAPTER 5: GOD'S MESSENGERS

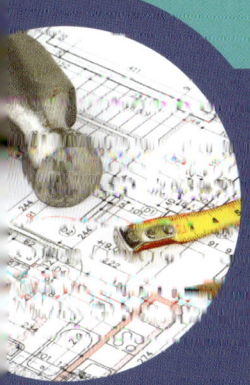

# Zechariah

**What It's About:** The Jewish people are commanded to get busy rebuilding the Temple—and watch for the arrival of their Messiah.

**Important Characters/People:** Zechariah, Zerubbabel, Joshua, Darius, Heldai, Tobijah, Jedaiah

**The Writer:** Zechariah, who is identified in the Bible as the son of Berekiah (1:1), wrote most or all of the book of Zechariah, but some experts believe a second, unnamed writer contributed chapters 9–14. This book was probably written between 520 and 475 BC.

## What You'll Find in Zechariah

**Like Haggai, Zechariah** preached to the people of Judah after their return from Babylon. Also like Haggai, Zechariah's words were written and spoken to encourage the people to dedicate themselves to finishing the new Temple.

Zechariah preached a message of encouragement, for the Temple would one day be home to the Messiah Himself. The first eight chapters of this prophecy focus on the need to finish the project, while the last six focus on the blessings in store for the Jewish people once the task is completed.

### FUN BIBLE TRIVIA

Zechariah's prophecy of the Messiah riding a donkey into Jerusalem (9:9) was fulfilled perfectly in Jesus' "triumphal entry" (Matthew 21:1–11). Also, the prophecy "They will look on me whom they have pierced" (12:10) refers to the Roman soldier's spearing of Christ after the Crucifixion (John 19:34).

DISCOVER THE BIBLE

# Malachi

**What It's About:** God warns the Jewish people to be more careful with their attitude toward Him and what He had told them to do.

**Important Characters/People:** Malachi, Persian rulers, Jewish religious leaders

**The Writer:** Other than what is in his book, not a lot is known about the prophet Malachi. He lived during the time of Nehemiah and Ezra, but he is not mentioned in the books of Nehemiah or Ezra. The book of Malachi was written between 440 and 400 BC.

## What You'll Find in the Book of Malachi

> **POWER WORDS**
>
> *"Bring all the tithes into the storehouse so there will be enough food in my Temple. If you do," says the LORD of Heaven's Armies, "I will open the windows of heaven for you. I will pour out a blessing so great you won't have enough room to take it in! Try it! Put me to the test!"*
>
> Malachi 3:10

**The words in** the book of Malachi are directed toward the Jews in Jerusalem about 100 years after the end of the Babylonian Captivity. The people were doing what they thought God wanted them to do, but in their hearts they had strayed from God.

Sadly, they were doing the same things and committing the same sins that had led to their captivity in the first place! The men were divorcing their wives to marry foreign women, the people weren't giving of their income the way God had instructed them, and the priests weren't giving God the best when they offered the required sacrifices.

God wanted His people to know how much He loved them, but He wanted them to see that they weren't returning that love. So, speaking through Malachi, God called the people to return to true worship and true love of God.

# CHAPTER 6

# The Bible's Main Man

The Story of Jesus (Matthew through John)

**The time between** the writing of the final book of the Old Testament—Malachi—and the birth of Jesus is sometimes called "the silent years," simply because God did not speak through prophets during those 400 years.

But God finally broke the silence with the arrival of the long-awaited Messiah, Jesus Christ. The story of His life is told in what are called the Gospels, the four books you'll read about in this chapter.

As you read through the Gospels, the first four books of the New Testament, you'll notice that they cover many of the same events in the life of Jesus. Even so, from one book to the next, the events may look very different—at least at first. Some of the Gospels include information you won't find in the others. Likewise, some Gospels leave out events that are included in one or more of the other Gospels.

That's because the Gospels were written by men with different life experiences and different ways of looking at things. What was really important to one writer may not have been as important to the others. When they wrote their Gospels, they focused on the things about Jesus' life they thought were most important—or most important to their readers.

Now, let's take a look at what you'll find in the four Gospels, starting where the New Testament starts: with the Gospel of Matthew.

>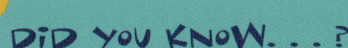
> **DID YOU KNOW. . . ?**
>
> The four Gospels included in the Bible (Matthew, Mark, Luke, and John) were not the only stories of the life and ministry of Jesus written during the first and second centuries. Far from it! Dozens and dozens of "gospels" were written during that time, and Christian leaders discussed—and often disagreed about—which ones were accurate accounts and which were not. The four Gospels in the Bible today were approved for inclusion at meetings—called councils—of Christian leaders in the fourth century.

## DISCOVER THE BIBLE

# The Gospel of Matthew

**What It's About:** The apostle Matthew writes about the things Jesus did and the words He spoke—and how they fulfilled Old Testament prophecies.

**Important Characters/People:** Jesus, Mary and Joseph, the wise men from the East, John the Baptist, Herod, the centurion, the 12 apostles

**The Writer:** Most Bible experts agree that the writer of the Gospel of Matthew was Matthew (also known as Levi), one of Jesus' 12 original disciples. Luke 5:27–28 tells us that Matthew left everything to follow Jesus when Jesus called him. Some experts believe that Matthew wrote his Gospel between AD 60 and 65, but others believe he wrote it as many as 20 years later.

### POWER WORDS

*"Love your enemies! Pray for those who persecute you! In that way, you will be acting as true children of your Father in heaven. For he gives his sunlight to both the evil and the good, and he sends rain on the just and the unjust alike."*

Matthew 5:44–45

### WHO, WHAT, WHERE?

If you were going to pick someone to write the story of Jesus' life and ministry here on earth, it probably wouldn't be a guy like Matthew. Before Jesus called him to be a disciple, Matthew was a tax collector for the hated Roman government—a job that most Jews despised because the tax collectors worked for the Romans and engaged in dishonest business practices.

## What You'll Find in the Gospel of Matthew

The Gospel of Matthew contains a lot of great messages for any Christian, but it was written specifically for the Jewish people of Matthew's time, especially to the first Jewish Christians.

For centuries, the Jews had suffered under foreign rule, and many of them were more than ready for their Messiah to come. Though Jesus wasn't exactly what most of the people expected, He was everything the Old Testament prophets said He would be.

Many times over, Matthew points out to his readers the things that Jesus did or said that fulfilled Old Testament prophecies about the coming Messiah. His Gospel quotes about 60 references to Old Testament prophecies and directly quotes the Old Testament about 40 times.

As you read the Gospel of Matthew, you'll notice that he uses the word *fulfilled* many times. Here are a few examples:

CHAPTER 6: THE BIBLE'S MAIN MAN

- "Joseph obeyed. He got up, took the child and his mother under cover of darkness. They were out of town and well on their way by daylight. They lived in Egypt until Herod's death. This Egyptian exile *fulfilled* what Hosea had preached. 'I called my son out of Egypt'" (2:14 MSG).
- "That evening a lot of demon-afflicted people were brought to him. He relieved the inwardly tormented. He cured the bodily ill. He *fulfilled* Isaiah's well-known sermon: He took our illnesses, He carried our diseases" (8:16 MSG).
- "All Jesus did that day was tell stories—a long storytelling afternoon. His storytelling *fulfilled* the prophecy: I will open my mouth and tell stories; I will bring out into the open things hidden since the world's first day" (13:34 the MSG).
- "All this was done that it might be *fulfilled* which was spoken by the prophet, saying: 'Tell the daughter of Zion, "Behold, your King is coming to you, lowly, and sitting on a donkey, a colt, the foal of a donkey"'" (21:4–5 NKJV).
- "Then they crucified Him, and divided His garments, casting lots, that it might be *fulfilled* which was spoken by the prophet: 'They divided My garments among them, and for My clothing they cast lots'" (27:35 NKJV).

> **POWER WORDS**
>
> "Keep on asking, and you will receive what you ask for. Keep on seeking, and you will find. Keep on knocking, and the door will be opened to you. For everyone who asks, receives. Everyone who seeks, finds. And to everyone who knocks, the door will be opened."
>
> Matthew 7:7–8

In a nutshell, Matthew's message for his audience was this: "Brothers and sisters, Jesus—the man I spent more than three years of my life with—is the Messiah we have been waiting for. But don't just take my word for it. Look at scripture and you'll see that His words and actions, as well as the things that happened to Him, prove who He is!"

The Gospel of Matthew starts out by referring to Jesus as "the son of David" NIV (the first fulfillment of prophecy that Matthew points out) and then traces Jesus' family tree from Abraham all the way through the centuries (and 14 generations) to Jesus' earthly father, Joseph. It then records the story of Jesus' birth and childhood (1:18–2:23), the ministry of John the Baptist (3:1–12), Jesus' baptism (3:13–17), His temptation by the devil (4:1–11), the calling of some of His disciples (4:12–22), and the beginning of His earthly ministry.

DISCOVER THE BIBLE

## The Best Sermon Ever Preached!

**Matthew is the** only Gospel to include a fairly long and very detailed set of Jesus' teachings called the Sermon on the Mount (even though Luke 6:17–49 is a shortened version of the same teaching). In chapters 5–7, you can read about some tough—but very practical—teachings by Jesus on a wide variety of subjects.

If you want to know what Jesus had to say about what God wants you to be, how He wants you to approach Him, and how you are to treat other people, take some time to read Matthew 5–7. And don't miss out on what Jesus had to say about prayer in Matthew 7:7–12.

### WHAT'S IN IT FOR ME?

The Sermon on the Mount starts out with eight statements called Beatitudes, which means "statements of blessing":
"Blessed are the poor in spirit, for theirs is the kingdom of heaven" (Matthew 5:3 NKJV).
"Blessed are those who mourn, for they shall be comforted" (Matthew 5:4 NKJV).
"Blessed are the meek, for they shall inherit the earth" (Matthew 5:5 NKJV).
"Blessed are those who hunger and thirst for righteousness, for they shall be filled" (Matthew 5:6 NKJV).
"Blessed are the merciful, for they shall obtain mercy" (Matthew 5:7 NKJV).
"Blessed are the pure in heart, for they shall see God" (Matthew 5:8 NKJV).
"Blessed are the peacemakers, for they shall be called sons of God" (Matthew 5:9 NKJV).
"Blessed are those who are persecuted for righteousness' sake, for theirs is the kingdom of heaven" (Matthew 5:10 NKJV).

CHAPTER 6: THE BIBLE'S MAIN MAN

# The Gospel of Mark

**What It's About:** This Gospel tells how Jesus proved that He is the Savior of all people, not just the Jews, by serving others, by suffering, by dying, and by being raised from the dead.

**Important Characters/People:** Jesus, John the Baptist, Herod, Pontius Pilate, the 12 apostles, the women who followed Jesus, the Pharisees

**The Writer:** The Gospel of Mark does not name its writer, but it is generally agreed that the writer was John Mark, who wasn't one of the original 12 disciples but who was a close associate of the apostle Peter. It is believed that John Mark received from Peter an eyewitness account of everything that appears in this Gospel. The Gospel of Mark was probably written around AD 57, making it one of the oldest books—if not *the* oldest book—of the New Testament.

## What You'll Find in the Gospel of Mark

**The Gospel of** Mark is the shortest of the four Gospels. That's because Mark left out a lot of details you'll find in the other Gospels—especially Matthew and Luke. For example, Mark doesn't mention anything at all about Jesus' family tree, and he doesn't mention anything about the virgin birth. Also missing is any part of the famous Sermon on the Mount, which is covered in three chapters in Matthew and one in Luke.

Even though this book tells basically the same story as Matthew, one of the things you might notice is that it doesn't focus on how Jesus fulfilled Old Testament prophecies. In fact, Mark quotes the Old Testament only twice. This is because Mark wasn't writing to a Jewish audience the way Matthew was. Instead, he was writing to Gentile (non-Jewish) Christians, who wouldn't have been as concerned about Old Testament prophecies as their Jewish brothers and sisters.

> **POWER WORDS**
> 
> *Jesus called out to them, "Come, follow me, and I will show you how to fish for people!"*
> 
> Mark 1:17

# DISCOVER THE BIBLE

### FUN BIBLE TRIVIA
Mark 14:51–52 tells us that, on the night when Jesus was arrested in the Garden of Gethsemane, a young follower of his escaped naked from the scene after having a linen garment pulled off of him. Some experts believe that young man was John Mark, the writer of the Gospel of Mark.

Mark understood what Jesus taught during His time on earth—and what the Old Testament prophecies about Jesus said: that Jesus was the Messiah or Savior, not just for the Jews+ but for people of all races.

As you read this book, you'll see that Jesus didn't just talk about serving others and sacrificing Himself for them—He put actions behind those words. After introducing his readers to Jesus with an account of His baptism by John the Baptist in the Jordan River, Mark writes about Jesus' life, death, and resurrection. Mark includes some of Jesus' teaching—including some of the parables—but he focuses more on the things Jesus did.

Starting in chapter 11, Mark's Gospel tells the story of Jesus' arrival in Jerusalem, where He would spend most of the last week of His life on earth. Chapters 11–13 cover Jesus' teaching and actions in the city of Jerusalem before His arrest and crucifixion. During that time, He also dealt with people who didn't like what He was doing and teaching and who wanted to kill Him because of His words and actions. He also taught His disciples about the things that would happen in the future (chapter 13).

Chapters 14 and 15 tell the story of Jesus' suffering and death, and chapter 16 covers His resurrection and some of the things He did and said before He returned to heaven to be with His Father.

# The Gospel of Luke

**What It's About:** Luke writes about how God's offer of salvation through Jesus is available to all people, not just the Jews. The Gospel of Luke focuses on Jesus as a perfect man—as the One who was fully God but also fully human. . . and perfect as both. In Luke, we can see Jesus as a man of amazing love and compassion for people around Him.

**Important Characters/People:** Jesus, Mary and Joseph, Zacharias and Elizabeth, the shepherds, Anna, Simeon, the 12 disciples, the Pharisees, Pilate, Herod

**The Writer:** Luke was a physician, historian, writer, and missionary, who accompanied the apostle Paul on his third of three missionary journeys. Luke was not one of Jesus' original disciples or even an eyewitness to His life here on earth. It isn't known for certain when he became a Christian. Luke is the only Gentile (non-Jew) to write a book of the Bible—in fact, he wrote two: the Gospel of Luke and the book of Acts. Luke probably wrote his Gospel between AD 58 and 65.

CHAPTER 6: THE BIBLE'S MAIN MAN

# What You'll Find in the Gospel of Luke

**Luke's Gospel is** the only one of the four that is written *chronologically*, meaning in the order that everything happened. It is written to someone named Theophilus (his name means "lover of God"). Luke begins his Gospel by explaining to Theophilus that he had investigated all the accounts written in the book.

Luke was apparently quite the historian, because his Gospel includes a lot of information not included in the other Gospels. For example, Luke gives his readers a detailed story of Jesus' birth—as well as the birth of John the Baptist. Many of the stories you hear told around Christmastime come from Luke's Gospel—including the angel's announcement to the shepherds that their Messiah had been born. (You can read that story in Luke 2:8–20.)

Luke also is the only Gospel writer to include anything about Jesus' childhood. In Luke, you can read about Jesus' circumcision, His presentation at the Temple, His visit with a godly man named Simeon and a prophetess named Anna, and the way He amazed Jewish religious scholars with His understanding when he was only 12 years old. (You can read these stories in Luke 2:21–52.)

### WHO, WHAT, WHERE?

The angel named Gabriel, who appeared to Mary to tell her she would be the mother of the Messiah (see Luke 1:26–38), is also mentioned in Daniel 9. Gabriel and Michael are the only angels mentioned by name in the Bible. Gabriel's name means "champion of God."

### POWER WORDS

*"Seek the Kingdom of God above all else, and he will give you everything you need."*

Luke 12:31

89

## DISCOVER THE BIBLE

### Who, What, Where?
Golgotha, also known in Latin as "Calvary," is mentioned in Luke 23:33 as the place where the Romans executed criminals. Jesus was crucified there. Golgotha, which means "skull," is not far outside the city of Jerusalem.

Luke's Gospel includes 25 parables—stories Jesus told to illustrate important truths about the kingdom of God—including 17 that appear only in his Gospel. Two of Jesus' most famous parables—the good Samaritan (10:25–37) and the prodigal son (15:11–32)—appear only in Luke. He also records seven miracles of Jesus that aren't found in the other three Gospels.

Luke presents Jesus as a man who showed compassion to all people, including some the Jewish people of that time wanted nothing to do with. That includes the poor (6:20), Roman soldiers (7:1–10), widows (7:11–17), the "sinful" (7:36–50), the sick (8:43–48), Samaritans (10:33), lepers (17:11–19), and many others—including a dying thief on a cross beside Him (23:40–43).

Jesus is also seen in Luke as a man who valued women in His ministry. For example, in chapter 1, Mary and Elizabeth play important roles in the story, and in chapter 10, He visits the home of Mary and Martha of Bethany. Like the other three Gospel writers, Luke wrote about Jesus' death and resurrection. He also added detailed accounts of Jesus' appearances to two believers on the Emmaus road and the 11 remaining disciples. At the end of Luke's Gospel, Jesus ascends to heaven to be with His Father.

# The Gospel of John

**What It's About:** Jesus is God in the flesh—the Son of God—and the Savior of all people.

**Important Characters/People:** Jesus, John the Baptist, the Samaritan woman at the well, Mary Magdalene, Lazarus, Mary and Martha of Bethany, Pilate

**Who Wrote It:** The writer of the fourth Gospel is the apostle John, the brother of the apostle James. (Don't get him mixed up with John the Baptist.) John and James were the sons of a fisherman named Zebedee, and they were two of Jesus' original 12 disciples. In his Gospel, John refers to himself as "the disciple whom Jesus loved." John's Gospel was the last one of the four written. It was completed between AD 80 and 100. Experts believe John wrote his Gospel when he was very old, while he lived in a Greek city called Ephesus, where he served as a leader of the Ephesian church.

CHAPTER 6: THE BIBLE'S MAIN MAN

# What You'll Find in the Gospel of John

**The apostle John** wastes no time in telling his readers what his Gospel is all about: "In the beginning was the Word, and the Word was with God, and the Word was God" (John 1:1 NKJV). The "Word" whom John wrote about is Jesus, and John wanted his readers to know that Jesus was no ordinary man and that He wasn't just a great teacher—He was God in the flesh!

The Gospel of John is different from the other three (Matthew, Mark, and Luke, which are called "synoptic Gospels" because they focus on many of the same events) in several important ways. John left out all of Jesus' parables and recorded only seven of His miracles.

John's Gospel focuses more on the spiritual part of Jesus' life and works. John records Jesus' explanation for coming to earth and His discussion of His relationship with God. As you read the Gospel of John, you'll notice that Jesus is often quoted as telling people that God had sent Him and that God was His Father.

John didn't include any of Jesus' parables in his Gospel, but he included some of Jesus' best-known miracles. In chapter 2, you can read the account of Jesus turning water into wine at a wedding in a place called Cana. Chapter 9 includes the story of Jesus healing a man who had been born blind and His teaching about that healing, and chapter 11 tells the story of Jesus raising His good friend Lazarus from the dead.

More than half of John's Gospel is devoted to the events of Jesus' life and teaching during His final week on earth. John records how, just hours before Jesus' arrest, He spoke to the disciples and gave them some final words of encouragement. Jesus told them:

- They should not be troubled by what was happening but to trust in Him (14:1–4).
- They were to trust in Him as the One whom God had sent (14:5–14).
- They were to continue obeying Him—with the help of the Holy Spirit (14:15–31).

## FUN BIBLE TRIVIA

John and his brother James, along with Peter, were part of what is called Jesus' "inner circle" of disciples. These three men were the closest to Jesus and often accompanied Him to places and events the others weren't allowed to see. For example, they were the only three allowed to be with Jesus at an event called the Transfiguration. (You can read that story in Matthew 17:1–9; Mark 9:2–10; and Luke 9:28–36.)

## POWER WORDS

*"For God loved the world so much that he gave his one and only Son, so that everyone who believes in him will not perish but have eternal life."*
John 3:16

91

## DISCOVER THE BIBLE

- They were to "abide" (remain) in Him (15:1–8).
- They were to love one another just as He had loved them (15:9–17).
- He would ask the Father to send the Holy Spirit to them (15:26–16:16).
- Their sadness would be turned to joy (16:17–28).

### WHO, WHAT, WHERE?

Jesus spoke the words of John 3:16—probably the best-known verse in the whole Bible—to a Jewish religious leader named Nicodemus, who visited Him late one night to find out more about Him. While most of the religious leaders of that time opposed Jesus, Nicodemus stood up for Him when they hatched the plan to arrest Him. Nicodemus also provided the expensive spices used on Jesus' body when He was buried.

Like the other three Gospels, John's includes the story of the apostle Peter's denial that he was one of Jesus' followers after Jesus was arrested. But John is the only Gospel writer to include the scene where Jesus spoke to Peter, forgave him, and invited him to continue following Him. (You can read that story in John 21:15–23.)

Now that we've covered the four written accounts of Jesus' life, let's take a look at the men who took His message to the world after Jesus returned to heaven. You'll find their stories in the next book in the Bible: the Acts of the Apostles, or simply Acts.

### DID YOU KNOW...?

Even though the Gospel of John is now many Christians' favorite Gospel, there was a time when church leaders questioned whether it should have been included in the Bible. Some even thought that John's Gospel included false teaching! But it was eventually accepted as part of the canon of scripture, even though many didn't believe it belonged there.

# CHAPTER 7

## How the Church Got Its Start

(Acts of the Apostles)

**The first four** books of the New Testament—Matthew through John—tell the wonderful story of how Jesus came to earth from heaven, was born to a virgin girl named Mary in a town called Bethlehem, lived and ministered among the Jewish people of that time, died on a cross, and was raised from the dead. That sounds like a great ending to the story, doesn't it? But there's more. Lots more! When we continue on from the end of John's Gospel and begin in the next New Testament book, the Acts of the Apostles (Acts for short), we read about how God started what is called "the Church" with a group of 120 believers gathered in Jerusalem, and then used some brave, dedicated men and women to spread the Good News of Jesus throughout the known world of that time.

Let's take a look at the book of Acts and the amazing story it has to tell.

## Acts

**What It's About:** Jesus' promise of the Holy Spirit comes true, and believers receive the power He told the apostles they would receive. The Church gets its start in Jerusalem and then spreads all over the known world.

**Important Characters/People:** Peter, John, Gamaliel, Stephen, Philip, Aquila and Priscilla, Paul, Barnabas, Herod, Agrippa, Festus, Apollos, Silas, Lydia, Luke, Timothy

**The Writer:** The book of Acts was written by Luke, the same writer who wrote the Gospel of Luke. Just as he did with his Gospel, Luke wrote Acts to a man named Theophilus (but the Bible gives us no other information about Theophilus)

# What You'll Find in the Book of Acts

**Acts picks up** almost exactly where the Gospel of Luke leaves off. The risen Jesus appeared to the apostles several times during the 40 days He remained on earth after God raised Him from the dead.

Not long after those 40 days had passed, Jesus appeared to the apostles one more time at a place called the Mount of Olives, which was located just outside the city of Jerusalem. He reminded them of His promise that God would send the Holy Spirit to give them power so that they could boldly tell the world around them about salvation through Jesus. After that, Jesus was "taken up into a cloud while they were watching, and they could no longer see him" (Acts 1:9).

## What Now?

**After Jesus returned** to heaven, that group of 120 believers, including the apostles, continued to meet together, waiting for God to do something amazing. God never disappoints someone who waits for Him, and that first group of believers was no exception!

One day, about seven weeks after Jesus was raised from the dead, while that small group of believers was gathered in a house in Jerusalem, the Holy Spirit came. It was an amazing scene! What looked like tongues of fire appeared and rested on each person in the room. Everyone there was filled with God's Spirit, and they began talking in languages they didn't even know!

### POWER WORDS
"You will receive power when the Holy Spirit comes upon you. And you will be my witnesses, telling people about me everywhere—in Jerusalem, throughout Judea, in Samaria, and to the ends of the earth."
Acts 1:8

### POWER WORDS
"Each of you must repent of your sins and turn to God, and be baptized in the name of Jesus Christ for the forgiveness of your sins. Then you will receive the gift of the Holy Spirit."
Acts 2:38

### DID YOU KNOW. . . ?
The word *apostle* comes from a Greek word meaning "one sent forth"—specifically to be a representative for the message of salvation through Jesus.

# CHAPTER 7: HOW THE CHURCH GOT ITS START

Not long after that, Peter—the same Peter who just weeks before was too scared to admit that he even knew Jesus—delivered an amazing sermon. When he was finished, that small group of 120 Christians was now a much bigger group—more than 3,000 people!

This gathering of believers called the Church continued to grow in numbers, mostly through the preaching of Peter and John. There were lots of miracles taking place, a few problems to solve, and some of the apostles got themselves in trouble with the local authorities. But through it all, the Church continued to grow, with new members being added every day.

But now it was time for the message of Jesus to spread from the cozy confines of Jerusalem.

> **POWER WORDS**
>
> "There is salvation in no one else! God has given no other name under heaven by which we must be saved."
>
> Acts 4:12

## You Can't Keep a Good Message Down (Acts 7–8)

**As the Church** continued to grow, both the Jewish religious leaders and the Roman government wondered what this new group was all about. Jesus had told the apostles that Christians would have to suffer terrible treatment because of Him. Up until now, however, the worst that had happened was that some of the apostles had been arrested for preaching about Jesus.

That all changed in a big way one day when a brave Christian named Stephen spoke to a group of Jewish religious leaders and told them things they didn't like to hear. He told them how Jesus was the Messiah they had been waiting for but that they had rejected Him.

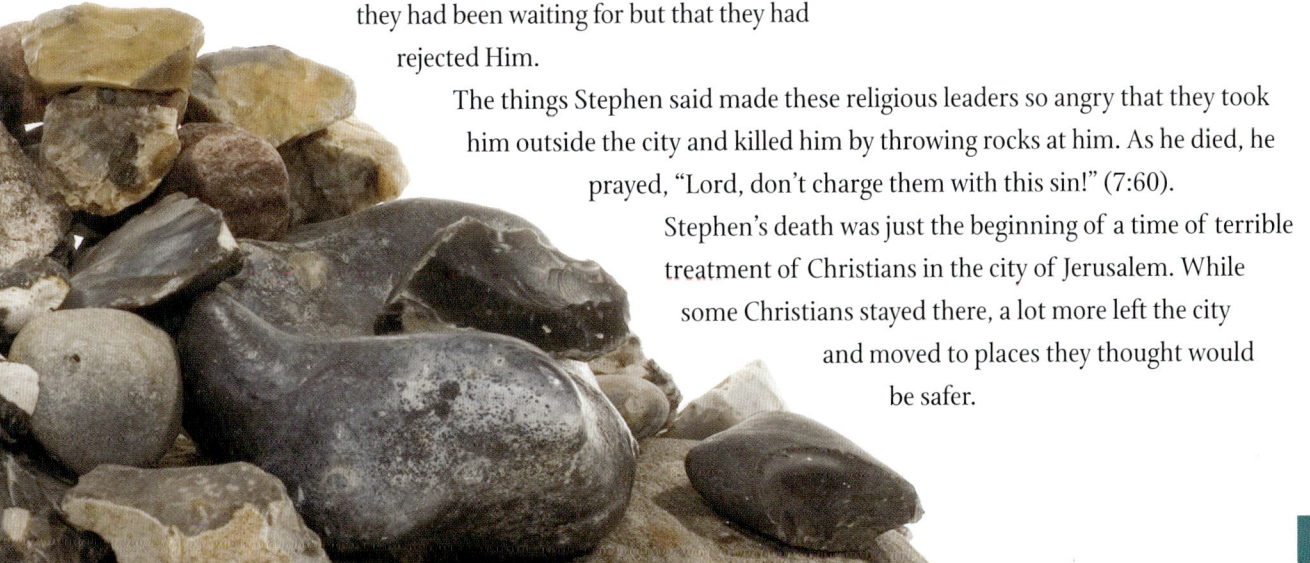

The things Stephen said made these religious leaders so angry that they took him outside the city and killed him by throwing rocks at him. As he died, he prayed, "Lord, don't charge them with this sin!" (7:60).

Stephen's death was just the beginning of a time of terrible treatment of Christians in the city of Jerusalem. While some Christians stayed there, a lot more left the city and moved to places they thought would be safer.

95

## DISCOVER THE BIBLE

### WHAT'S IN IT FOR ME?

While there was nothing good or right about what happened to Stephen, he is an example of how God can take the bad things that happen to a Christian and use them for good. You probably won't have to suffer something like what Stephen suffered, but how do you respond when bad things happen to you?

You might think that when the Christians began to suffer it would bring about the end of Christianity in that part of the world; but it turned out to be only the beginning. You see, when the Christians left Jerusalem, they took with them their faith, and many of them preached to people in places like Judea and Samaria.

## Paul: Jesus' Most Unlikely Servant

**The Christians in** Jerusalem suffered through terrible treatment. Some had their property taken away, some were beaten, and some even lost their lives.

One of the men responsible for this persecution was a Jewish religious leader named Saul (later called Paul). In chapter 9 of Acts, we read how Saul was on his way from Jerusalem to a city called Damascus to attack the Christians there. But something happened to Saul on the road to Damascus—something that would lead to the spread of Christianity all over the world.

As Saul neared Damascus, a bright light came from heaven, so intense that it blinded him and caused him to fall to the ground, and a voice said to him, "Saul! Saul! Why are you persecuting me?" (9:4).

It was Jesus talking to Saul!

Jesus told Paul to go to Damascus and wait for further instructions. Three days after Saul arrived in Damascus, he miraculously received his sight back. But more important than that, he received the Holy Spirit. He would never be the same again!

### FUN BIBLE TRIVIA

The first time the word *Christians* appears in the Bible is in Acts 11:26, which says that the believers in Antioch were the first to be called Christians. Some experts believe this word may have been used by nonbelievers back then in a negative or mocking way, but it has stuck as a title for people who follow Jesus.

# CHAPTER 7: HOW THE CHURCH GOT ITS START

If you think some of the Christians who heard that Saul was God's choice to preach the gospel to the non-Jewish world were a little skeptical, you'd be right! Ananias, who took care of Saul during his first three days in Damascus, could hardly believe his ears when God told him that Saul would preach to Gentiles, kings, and the people of Israel. But Ananias took care of Saul, just as God had told him to do, making him an important part of the story. (You can read the whole story in Acts 9:10–19.)

The Christians in Jerusalem were also a little wary of Saul. In fact, when he first showed up to meet with them in Jerusalem, they were afraid of him! They thought he was only pretending to be a Christian and that he had something up his sleeve. But after they found out how he had met Jesus on the road to Damascus and how he had so courageously preached there afterward, they accepted him as one of their own.

### WHO, WHAT, WHERE?

When we first meet Paul in the Bible, he is watching the stoning of Stephen and giving his approval. Later in the book of Acts, we find more details about Paul's life before he started attacking Christians. For example, he was born in a Roman city called Tarsus (22:3), he was a Pharisee and the son of a Pharisee (23:6), he studied Jewish law under a teacher named Gamaliel (22:3), he was a citizen of Rome (22:25–28), and he had a sister who lived in Jerusalem (23:16).

## A New Name...and a Road Trip

**When you get** to Acts 13:9, the first thing you will probably notice is that something else had changed about Saul: his name! This is the first time the Bible calls the man formerly known as Saul by the name Paul.

Chapter 13 of Acts records the beginning of the first of three journeys Paul took during his lifetime to preach the message of Jesus. By this time, Antioch, a city in Syria, had replaced Jerusalem as the Church's headquarters.

Paul began this trip with a man named Barnabas and with a young assistant named John Mark, who was a relative of Barnabas's. This long road trip took about three years and is covered in Acts 13:1–15:35.

### POWER WORDS

"We are here to proclaim that through this man Jesus there is forgiveness for your sins. Everyone who believes in him is declared right with God—something the law of Moses could never do."
Acts 13:38-39

97

DISCOVER THE BIBLE

## WHAT'S IN IT FOR ME?

Acts 13:13 tells the story of a young man named John Mark, who deserted Paul and Barnabas during Paul's first missionary journey. Quitting and going home wasn't a great way to start out a life of ministry, but John Mark finished strong. He even wrote a book that ended up in the Bible: the Gospel of Mark. If you've ever failed at something or even quit when things got tough, you don't have to let that failure stop you from doing great things for God.

After a time of fasting and prayer, the three men set sail for the island of Cyprus, Barnabas's home, where they traveled from town to town preaching the gospel (13:1–4). From there, they moved on to Perga. It was here that John Mark left them and returned to Jerusalem. After that, Paul and Barnabas traveled to a town called Pisidian Antioch, where they established the world's first Gentile church.

During the rest of the trip, Paul and Barnabas saw a lot of people coming to faith in Jesus, but they also had to run for their lives a few times. In one city, Lystra (14:8–19), Paul and Barnabas were treated as gods after they performed a miracle healing; but then they were nearly stoned to death after people came from other cities and stirred up the crowds against them.

Their last stop was a city called Derbe (14:20–21), where many people came to faith in Jesus. On their return trip to Antioch, they revisited some of the places they'd been before, and this time they appointed leaders in the newly formed churches (14:21–26).

CHAPTER 7: HOW THE CHURCH GOT ITS START

# Road Trip, Part 2 (Acts 15:36–18:22)

**After hanging out** in Antioch for a while, Paul set out on his second missionary journey. This time, he traveled with a new partner, a man named Silas. The plan was to have Paul, Barnabas, and Silas travel together, but when Paul and Barnabas disagreed over whether or not to take John Mark with them again (Paul was against the idea), they separated, leaving only Silas as Paul's traveling companion.

Along the way, Paul and Silas added two new members to their group: Timothy, who joined them while they were in Derbe and Lystra; and Luke, who joined them while they were in Troas, a Roman colony (see the Fun Bible Trivia sidebar on this page).

On one of their stops—a city called Philippi—Paul and Silas were beaten and thrown in jail. (You can read the whole story in Acts 16:13–40.) Then a miraculous earthquake shook the prison, giving the two men a chance to make their escape. Instead, they stayed put. Because they didn't escape, the jailer, who would have been in trouble if they had escaped, became a Christian.

### FUN BIBLE TRIVIA

During Paul's second missionary journey, Luke the physician—the same Luke who wrote the Gospel of Luke and the book of Acts—joined the team. We know this because, starting with Acts 16:10, Luke refers to the team as "we," meaning he was with them everywhere they went.

### DID YOU KNOW...?

On Paul's second missionary journey, he visited four cities that became homes to churches he later wrote letters to—letters that later became part of the New Testament. Those cities (and the books of the Bible they are named after) are Philippi (Philippians), Thessalonica (1 and 2 Thessalonians), Corinth (1 and 2 Corinthians), and Ephesus (Ephesians).

Paul and Silas were beaten and thrown in jail.

# DISCOVER THE BIBLE

## POWER WORDS

*"Believe in the Lord Jesus and you will be saved, along with everyone in your household."*
Acts 16:31

## WHO, WHAT, WHERE?

Acts 17:11-12 describes the people of Berea as "more open-minded" than the people of Thessalonica and as people who eagerly heard his message and searched the scriptures to see if what he said was true. Many Jews in Berea believed in Jesus as a result of their searching.

After leaving Philippi, Paul and Silas traveled to Thessalonica (17:1–4), Berea (17:10–12), Athens (17:16–33), Corinth (18:1–18), Ephesus (18:19–20), and Jerusalem (18:22). After making those stops, Paul and Silas returned to Antioch, Syria.

In Athens, which is now the capital city of Greece, Paul was sad to see all the idols erected to the Greek "gods." But when he saw one with an inscription that read, "To an Unknown God," he took the opportunity to tell the people about a God they could know through Jesus Christ.

Paul and Silas stayed in Corinth for about 18 months. While there, they met Aquila and Priscilla, a married couple who later traveled with Paul. Paul also wrote his two letters to the Thessalonians while he was in Corinth.

The Parthenon of Athens was dedicated to Athena, the Greek goddess of war, civilization, and justice.

Modern-day Athens, Greece

CHAPTER 7: HOW THE CHURCH GOT ITS START

## The First Two Trips Were So Good, We're Taking a Third (Acts 18:23–21:14)

**Paul's third and** final missionary journey was the longest of the three, beginning in about AD 53 and ending around AD 58.

After spending some time in Antioch, Paul set out to the cities in Galatia and Phrygia, including Tarsus and Iconium. He then traveled to Ephesus, where he stayed for almost three years (Acts 19:1–41).

God did a lot of great work through Paul in Ephesus. Paul preached and taught and did many great miracles—including healing the sick and casting out evil spirits (Acts 19:11–12). His work was so amazing that even magicians stopped their evil practices and burned very expensive books they used for their magic (Acts 19:17–20).

Later, Paul was nearly killed when he exposed the dishonesty of men who were in the business of making and selling idols (19:24–27). Even though Paul was a very busy man, he also found time to write his first letter to the Corinthian church and his letter to the Galatians, both of which are now in the Bible.

Paul then traveled to Macedonia and Greece (20:1–3), where he wrote his second letter to the Corinthians. From there he traveled to Troas (20:6–12) and then to Assos (20:13–14) and then back to Ephesus (20:17–35). The final three stops on his third missionary journey were in Tyre (21:3–6), Ptolemais (21:7), and Caesarea (21:8).

> **FUN BIBLE TRIVIA**
> In Acts 20:35, Paul quotes Jesus as saying, "It is more blessed to give than to receive." But don't try to find a verse that says that in the four Gospels. Even though that quote sounds a lot like something Jesus would have said, and Paul probably heard from one of the apostles that Jesus had said it, you won't find an account of Jesus speaking those words in Matthew, Mark, Luke, or John.

DISCOVER THE BIBLE

# On to Jerusalem and Rome (Acts 21:15–23:15)

**Who, What, Where?**
Malta, where the apostle Paul and others stayed after their ship wrecked on the way to Rome, is a southern European archipelago (a large group of islands) located in the Mediterranean Sea, about 60 miles south of the southeastern tip of Sicily, Italy.

**The last eight** chapters of the book of Acts take place after Paul's third and final missionary journey. But that doesn't mean Paul was finished preaching and teaching the Good News about Jesus. And it also doesn't mean an end to the threats on his life.

Even though Paul had been warned there would be trouble if he traveled to Jerusalem, he still went there. This time, the Christians in Jerusalem welcomed him, but his reception among the Jews in the city wasn't as friendly. He was arrested in the Temple after a riot broke out because of the things he preached (21:26–36).

After Paul learned of a plot to kill him, he was sent to Caesarea, where he stayed two years before he was sent to Rome. On the way to Rome, the ship he was sailing on shipwrecked during a terrible storm, and he ended up on the island of Malta, where he continued preaching. (You can read this story in Acts 27:14–28:10.)

When Paul finally arrived in Rome, he was placed under house arrest. He was allowed to live by himself—with a Roman soldier to guard him. During his two years in Rome, he wrote several more letters that were later included in the Bible: Ephesians, Philippians, two letters to Timothy, and Philemon.

While Paul was in Rome, he continued to preach—"boldly proclaiming the Kingdom of God and teaching about the Lord Jesus Christ. And no one tried to stop him" (28:31).

The Bible doesn't say exactly when Paul died or how. But historians teach that he was killed by the Roman emperor Nero around AD 67.

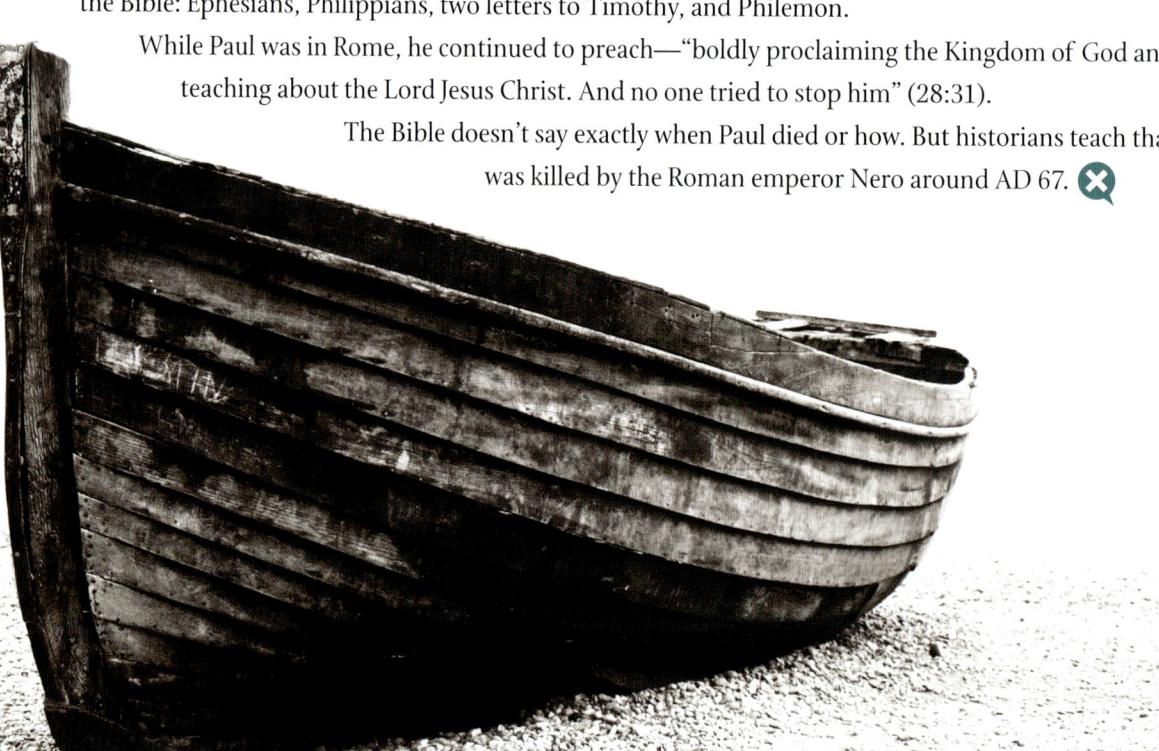

# Chapter 8

## Letters That Became Books of the Bible

**Epistles from Paul, Peter, and the Rest (Romans through Jude)**

**If you've ever** read through your Bible from Genesis to Revelation, right after you finished reading about the life, words, and deeds of Jesus Christ (Matthew through John), you moved on to the adventures of the men He appointed to continue His work in the then-known world (Acts).

If you're like a lot of people who have just finished reading the Gospels and the book of Acts, you might be wondering, *Okay, now that I know a little something about what Jesus and the men who followed Him have done, what does it mean to me?*

The next 21 books of the Bible—books that are called the Epistles—give you an amazing number of answers to that question. In these books, you'll find some very practical instructions on what you are to believe, how you are to live, and how you are to treat other people.

The Bible's epistles are actually personal letters written by men called apostles. At least five (and probably six) men wrote letters that ended up in the New Testament. The apostle Paul wrote most of the epistles included in the New Testament. He is known for certain to have written 13 of the letters (Romans, 1 and 2 Corinthians, Galatians, Ephesians, Philippians, Colossians, 1 and 2 Thessalonians, 1 and 2 Timothy, Titus, and Philemon) and is thought by some to have written Hebrews (more on that later).

### DID YOU KNOW...?

Though Paul is credited with writing the first 13 epistles in the New Testament, he didn't work alone. Romans 16:22 credits an assistant of Paul's named Tertius with helping the apostle write down his letter to the Roman Christians; and I Corinthians 1:1 credits a man named Sosthenes with assisting Paul in his first letter to the Christians in Corinth. Nothing else is known about either man.

DISCOVER THE BIBLE

# Romans

**What It's About:** The apostle Paul explains to the Roman Christians that everyone born since the days of Adam and Eve comes into this world as a sinner—someone who is not at peace with God. But there is a way of salvation—and only one way—and that's through faith in Jesus Christ.

**Important Characters/People:** Paul, Phoebe, Priscilla, Aquila, and many others mentioned in Romans 16

**The Writer:** Paul, with help from Tertius (16:22), wrote this letter in about AD 56, while he was in the city of Corinth.

## What You'll Find in the Book of Romans

### POWER WORDS

*And we know that God causes everything to work together for the good of those who love God and are called according to his purpose for them.*
Romans 8:28

**Romans is different** from Paul's letters to the other churches, because he wrote it to a church he'd never personally visited. In fact, he had never even seen the city of Rome at the time he wrote this letter. Paul hoped to see the Roman Christians face-to-face when he traveled to Spain (15:23–24). It's not known if Paul ever made it to Spain, but he did end up in Rome at the end of his life.

Some people have called Romans the "Gospel according to Paul," because it gives its readers such a detailed but simple plan for salvation.

The book of Romans starts out by describing in detail the sad condition of all people. In the first two chapters and most of the third, Paul writes about God's anger over human sin. He points out that even the best people in the world don't live the way God wants them to live. Not only that, but he writes that simply following God's written laws isn't enough to make us right with Him.

Modern-day Rome, Italy

# CHAPTER 8: LETTERS THAT BECAME BOOKS OF THE BIBLE

It seems like a pretty hopeless situation, but in chapter 3, Paul begins to explain why there is still hope. It's almost as if Paul were saying, "Here's the bad news, but stay with me while I tell you the Good News!" Sure, everyone sins and falls short of God's standard (3:23), but God Himself has lovingly provided the way for people to overcome that sin and have peace with Him: "Yet God, with undeserved kindness, declares that we are righteous. He did this through Christ Jesus when he freed us from the penalty for our sins" (3:24).

Paul wanted the Christians in Rome to understand that it wasn't about being a better person or about making an effort to follow God's rules. It's not that it wasn't a good idea to do those things, but they would never be enough to get a person into heaven. Salvation comes through one simple thing: trusting in Jesus Christ, who died as a sacrifice for our sins.

In chapters 6–8, Paul encourages his readers with the promise that they can live the way God wants them to live because God has given them power through the Holy Spirit. In chapters 9–11, he expands on how God worked His perfect plan to make people at peace with Him. Chapters 12–15 are some practical instructions for the Christian life.

### WHAT'S IN IT FOR ME?

Paul writes in Romans 8:15 that Christians can call God "Abba, Father." *Abba* is an Aramaic word for the word *father* that implies a really close relationship—kind of like when you call your father "Daddy." Paul uses this very same word to describe our relationship with God in Galatians 4:6.

# 1 Corinthians

**What It's About:** The people in the church in the city of Corinth weren't living the way Christians should live and weren't treating one another the way they should, so Paul wrote this letter to correct them and encourage them.

**Important Characters/People:** Paul, Apollos, Priscilla, Aquila, Timothy, Crispus, Sosthenes, Stephanas

**The Writer:** The apostle Paul, with help from Sosthenes (1:1)

DISCOVER THE BIBLE

# What You'll Find in the Book of 1 Corinthians

### POWER WORDS

Three things will last forever—faith, hope, and love—and the greatest of these is love.

1 Corinthians 13:13

### WHAT'S IN IT FOR ME?

Chapter 13 of 1 Corinthians is well known as the "love chapter" of the Bible. Take some time to read this chapter and ask yourself how you can better show your love for your family, friends, people at church, and others around you.

**Paul helped establish** the Corinthian church during his second missionary journey (Acts 18). But after Paul moved on to Ephesus, he found out that the Corinthians were having some serious problems. There were arguments in the church, ungodly living, and even lawsuits among the Christians there. Chapters 1–6 cover Paul's warnings and encouragements for the Christians at Corinth about unity in the church and right living for Christians.

In 1 Corinthians, Paul teaches on marriage (chapter 7), problems with food and idols (chapter 8), Christian freedom (chapter 9), the Lord's Supper (11:17–34), spiritual gifts (chapters 12–14), the resurrection of the dead (chapter 15), and giving (chapter 16).

# 2 Corinthians

**What It's About:** The apostle Paul writes another letter to the Corinthians, this time to defend his ministry.

**Important Characters/People:** Paul, the Corinthian church leaders, Titus

**The Writer:** The apostle Paul, with help from Timothy (1:1)

CHAPTER 8: LETTERS THAT BECAME BOOKS OF THE BIBLE

# What You'll Find in the Book of 2 Corinthians

**The Corinthian Christians** had dealt with some of the problems Paul wrote to them about in his first letter to them, but some troublemakers in Corinth questioned Paul's authority and attempted to divide the church. In the first seven chapters of 2 Corinthians, Paul describes his work as an apostle.

Chapters 8 and 9 of this book are Paul's instructions for giving and sharing in the church, including his words "God loves a person who gives cheerfully" (9:7). In the next three chapters, Paul defends his position as an apostle and tells the Corinthians why he writes with the authority he does.

### FUN BIBLE TRIVIA

In 2 Corinthians 12:7, Paul mentions a "thorn in my flesh" that God used to keep him humble. Paul doesn't say exactly what that "thorn" is, but some believe it might have been a physical problem like bad eyesight, migraine headaches, or epilepsy. Others believe it might have been attacks in the spiritual or human realm.

# Galatians

**What It's About:** Paul writes to the Galatian Christians to remind them to trust in only Jesus for their salvation and not in Jewish laws and customs. Paul wanted the Galatians to understand that the Christian life isn't about observing a lot of rules and regulations but about living under the power of the Holy Spirit.

**Important Characters/People:** Paul, Abraham, Sarah, Hagar, Ishmael, Isaac

**The Writer:** The apostle Paul. He wrote his letter to the Galatians around AD 50. This letter was actually written to several churches in a larger area called Galatia, which was located in Asia Minor (now Turkey).

## Discover the Bible

# What You'll Find in the Book of Galatians

> **POWER WORDS**
> *Clearly no one is justified before God by the law, because, "The righteous will live by faith."*
> Galatians 3:11 NIV

**The Galatian Christians** had started their lives of faith in Jesus well, but then a big problem came along. Men called "Judaizers" were trying to convince the Galatians, including the Gentiles, that they needed to observe Jewish rituals and customs in order to be true Christians.

Paul starts out his letter by telling the Galatians that he is shocked that they would turn way from God and His love and mercy (1:6) and follow a different path. He even writes of the Judaizers, "Let God's curse fall on anyone, including us or even an angel from heaven, who preaches a different kind of Good News than the one we preached to you" (1:8). Paul called the Galatian Christians "foolish Galatians" (3:1), because many of them had tried to take the salvation God had given them freely through Jesus Christ and add Jewish customs and rituals to it.

The main theme of the book of Galatians is *freedom*, and Paul wanted all Christians, including us today, to understand that because we have Jesus, we are free to love God and others without adding rituals, customs, or any human effort to our Christian lives.

# Ephesians

**What It's About:** Paul writes to the church in the city of Ephesus (in Asia Minor) to explain their true identity as Christians and what it should mean to them in their daily lives.

**Important Characters/People:** Paul, Timothy, Tychicus

**The Writer:** The apostle Paul

# What You'll Find in the Book of Ephesians

**If you want** to have a good understanding of what God has done for you through Jesus and who He says you are as a Christian, the book of Ephesians is a great place to start.

Paul started the church in Ephesus during his second missionary journey. (You can read the story in Acts 19.) Even though Paul had spent two years in the city, he later wrote to the Ephesians from his prison cell in Rome to explain

# CHAPTER 8: LETTERS THAT BECAME BOOKS OF THE BIBLE

the meaning of their relationship to Jesus Christ and how it should change their way of living and thinking.

The first three chapters of Ephesians teach what God has done in bringing people to Himself through Jesus. Paul told the Ephesians that through Jesus, God had brought both Jews and Gentiles together to Himself (2:11–18). The final three chapters explain what this new life in Jesus should look like—both in the church and in the home and other places.

## Who, What, Where?

Ephesus was the capital city of the Roman province of Asia, in the western part of Asia Minor (now Turkey). The Ephesian church is mentioned in the book of Revelation, where the apostle John wrote God's prophetic message praising the Ephesians for their good deeds but warning them that they had lost their first love (Revelation 2:1–7).

# Philippians

**What It's About:** Paul writes a heartfelt letter of love, friendship, and encouragement to the believers at the church in the city of Philipi.

**Important Characters/People:** Paul, Epaphroditus, Timothy, Euodia, Syntyche

**The Writer:** Paul, along with Timothy (1:1)

# What You'll Find in the Book of Philippians

**When you're going** through a hard time and are feeling a little sad, discouraged, or worried, then maybe you should crack your Bible open to the book of Philippians, one of the most positive, upbeat, encouraging books in the whole Bible.

The apostle Paul was probably sitting in a stinky, cold Roman prison cell when he wrote this letter. He had helped establish the Philippian church during his second missionary journey, and this letter shows that he had some very positive, warm feelings for the Christians there.

One of the things you'll notice as you read Philippians is that Paul uses the words *joy* and *rejoicing* over and over. That includes a verse you may have sung as a song at Sunday school: "Rejoice in the Lord always. Again I will say,

# DISCOVER THE BIBLE

### POWER WORDS
*Don't worry about anything; instead, pray about everything. Tell God what you need, and thank him for all he has done.*
Philippians 4:6

rejoice!" (4:4 NKJV). Paul knew for himself that no matter what kinds of circumstances he was in, he could always find joy in Jesus. He wanted the Christians in Philippi—and you—to understand that.

One thing Paul never says in this letter is that life is always going to be easy or fun. He was in a bad place himself (he knew his life could be nearing an end), and he warned the Philippians that they could expect to have to suffer for Jesus (1:29–30). Still, he wrote a book filled with words of joy for the life God had allowed him to live and the things God had allowed him to do.

## Colossians

**What It's About:** To fight against false teaching that had arisen in the church in Colossae, Paul writes to the Colossian Christians to remind them that Jesus is higher and greater than everything and everyone.

**Important Characters/People:** Paul, Barnabas, Aristarchus, Justus

**The Writer:** The apostle Paul, along with Timothy (1:1)

### DID YOU KNOW. . . ?
In Colossians 4:16, Paul mentions a letter he wrote to the church in Laodicea. This was one of probably dozens of letters Paul wrote that didn't make it into the Bible as part of the New Testament. Paul also asked that the letter to the Colossians be read to the Christians in Laodicea.

## What You'll Find in the Book of Colossians

**The Colossian church**—like so many others of that time—had been the target of false teaching (or, as Paul calls it in Colossians 2:4, "well-crafted arguments") that had caused some of the Christians in Colossae to add unhelpful things to their Christian faith. When Paul found out about the situation, he wrote this letter to remind the people that Jesus was all they needed—not additional rules and regulations, false thinking, angels, or anything else.

CHAPTER 8: LETTERS THAT BECAME BOOKS OF THE BIBLE

To demonstrate who Jesus is and what He meant to them, Paul reminded the Colossians that Jesus is the image of the invisible God (1:15), is the firstborn over all creation (1:15), is the creator of all things (1:16), is before all things (1:17), holds all things together (1:17), and is the head of the church (1:18).

### POWER WORDS

*Think about the things of heaven, not the things of earth.*

COLOSSIANS 3:2

# 1 Thessalonians

**What It's About:** Paul writes to the church in the Macedonian city of Thessalonica to instruct the Christians on living the way God wants them to live and also to assure them that Jesus will one day return to earth.

**Important Characters/People:** Paul, Silas, Timothy

**The Writer:** The apostle Paul, along with Silvanus (Silas) and Timothy (1:1). Paul, along with Silas, his traveling companion, had started the church in Thessalonica during his second missionary journey (Acts 17:1–9). He wrote his first letter to the Thessalonians around AD 50.

# What You'll Find in the Book of 1 Thessalonians

**The first three** chapters of this book are Paul's greetings and words of encouragement to a church he knew was growing strong in the faith. In chapter 4, he gives them instructions on living a godly life and encourages them with the promise that Jesus will return and Christians who have already died will go to heaven when He comes back.

### WHAT'S IN IT FOR ME?

The book of 1 Thessalonians contains many promises for you as a Christian—including the promise that because you are a Christian, you will one day be together in heaven with all your Christian family members and friends (4:13–18).

DISCOVER THE BIBLE

# 2 Thessalonians

**What It's About:** Paul writes a follow-up letter to the Thessalonian church to encourage them not just to wait around until Jesus returns, but to continue the work God has for them to do.

**Important Characters/People:** Paul, the "man of lawlessness"

**The Writer:** The apostle Paul, along with Silvanus (Silas) and Timothy (1:1)

## What You'll Find in the Book of 2 Thessalonians

**Paul wrote this** letter to help calm the shaken and troubled (2:2) Thessalonians, who had been told that Jesus had already returned to earth. Some of the Thessalonian Christians had quit their money-earning jobs and stopped doing the work God had for them to do here on earth.

In this letter, Paul assures them that Jesus' second coming is still in the future and that they should continue the work they had been doing before. In chapter 2, Paul tells the Thessalonians not to pay any attention to those who tell them Jesus has already returned and gives them an outline of what will take place in the "Day of the Lord." He explains that this day won't come until the "man of lawlessness" is revealed (2:8).

# 1 Timothy

**What It's About:** Paul's letter of instruction and encouragement for the church in Ephesus and to a young pastor named Timothy. In this letter, Paul gives Timothy the requirements for church leadership.

**Important Characters/People:** Paul, Timothy, church leaders, Hymenaeus, Alexander

**The Writer:** The apostle Paul

CHAPTER 8: LETTERS THAT BECAME BOOKS OF THE BIBLE

# What You'll Find in the Book of 1 Timothy

**The apostle Paul** wasn't just the greatest missionary in the history of Christianity, and he wasn't just the writer of many of the books in the New Testament. Paul was also a teacher and a mentor, and one of his students was Timothy, a young man who had been with Paul on his missionary journeys.

Paul begins his first letter to young Timothy by warning him against some of the false teaching that had made its way around the churches in that part of the world. He encourages Timothy to "fight well in the Lord's battles" and "cling to your faith in Christ, and keep your conscience clear" (1:18–19). In chapter 2, Paul lists some guidelines for the conduct of the church. Then, in chapter 3, he lists the qualifications for pastors and deacons, who were the church leaders of that time.

Chapters 4–6 cover a variety of topics, including more advice for church leaders, including Timothy himself (4:4–16), caring for widows (5:1–21), and avoiding the love of money (6:10–17).

### Who, What, Where?
Timothy was a young man who worked side by side with the apostle Paul, who assigned him the tough job of pastoring the church in Ephesus. In his letters to Timothy, Paul addresses him as a loving father would a son.

DISCOVER THE BIBLE

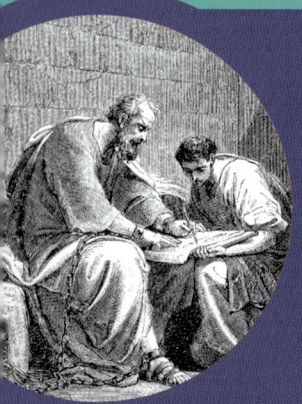

# 2 Timothy

**What It's About:** Paul's final words of encouragement to his much-loved partner and spiritual son, Timothy

**Important Characters/People:** Paul, Timothy, Demas, Crescens, Carpus, Titus, Luke, John Mark, Alexander

**The Writer:** The apostle Paul, who wrote this letter in approximately AD 67, shortly before he was put to death in Rome

### POWER WORDS

*For God saved us and called us to live a holy life. He did this, not because we deserved it, but because that was his plan from before the beginning of time.*
2 Timothy 1:9

### DID YOU KNOW...?

The first nine epistles in the New Testament were written to churches. The next four were written to individuals. Both letters to Timothy and the one to Titus were written to church leaders who had traveled with Paul. That is why they are sometimes called "pastoral epistles."

## What You'll Find in the Book of 2 Timothy

**Sitting in a** Roman prison cell, Paul wrote this letter to Timothy, his young friend and "true son in the faith" (1 Timothy 1:2). Paul knew his life was probably going to end soon, and he might have known that this letter would be his "last words." But even though Paul was in a terrible place, he didn't dwell on his own circumstances but took the time to express his concern for other Christians, especially Timothy.

In this letter, Paul encourages young Timothy to continue loving Jesus passionately and to preserve the truth he had learned from Paul. He pushes him to live the way God wants him to live as an example to Christians around him. Paul also warns Timothy to expect trouble as a result of living for Jesus (3:12) but also encourages him with the promise that God will always be faithful.

CHAPTER 8: LETTERS THAT BECAME BOOKS OF THE BIBLE

# Titus

**What It's About:** Paul instructs Christian leaders on how to live and how to lead their churches.

**Important Characters/People:** Paul, Titus

**The Writer:** The apostle Paul

## What You'll Find in the Book of Titus

**The apostle Paul** had left a young traveling companion named Titus on the Mediterranean island of Crete so that Titus could appoint church leaders and correct some of the problems in the new church there.

The people of Crete were known back then for their bad behavior, and they needed a strong leader who would hold them accountable for their actions. Titus was just that kind of leader.

Paul's letter to Titus encourages him to choose godly leaders and to set an example for the Christians on Crete by living the kind of life God wanted him to live. But this book applies to more than just church leaders—it gives good advice for any Christian to follow.

### Who, What, Where?

Titus was a Gentile (non-Jewish) friend and helper of the apostle Paul who accompanied Paul and Barnabas on a journey to Jerusalem (see Galatians 2:1) and who was with Paul during his imprisonment in Rome (2 Timothy 4:10). The Bible says he was completely selfless and trustworthy (2 Corinthians 12:18).

DISCOVER THE BIBLE

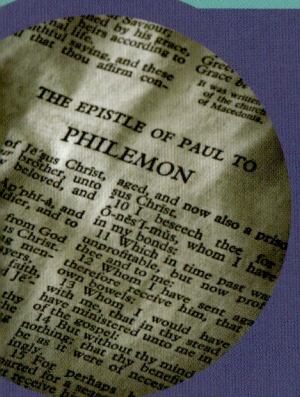

# Philemon

**What It's About:** Paul encourages a slave owner named Philemon to treat his runaway slave like he would any other fellow Christian: with love, compassion, and forgiveness.

**Important Characters/People:** Paul, Timothy, Philemon, Onesimus

**The Writer:** The apostle Paul. He wrote his letter to Philemon in about AD 60 while in prison in Rome.

### WHAT'S IN IT FOR ME?

The story of Philemon and his runaway slave is an example of how a Christian should treat someone who has done something wrong. Paul knows Philemon has every right under the law to have Onesimus harshly punished, but Paul begs his friend to treat Onesimus with forgiveness and compassion.

## What You'll Find in the Book of Philemon

**A slave named** Onesimus had robbed Philemon and run away to Rome, where he met Paul and became a Christian. Paul wanted to keep Onesimus in Rome as a helper, but because Philemon didn't approve, Paul sent Onesimus back to Colossae. Paul then writes a very personal letter in which he asks Philemon to forgive his runaway slave, who faced severe punishment under Roman law for running away from his master.

CHAPTER 8: LETTERS THAT BECAME BOOKS OF THE BIBLE

# Hebrews

**What It's About:** The writer of this letter shows his readers that Jesus is better than any Old Testament sacrifice or ritual. In fact, while those sacrifices and rituals were an imperfect way to approach God, Jesus provided the one and only perfect way to God.

**Important Characters/People:** Moses, Joshua, Melchizedek, the Hebrew patriarchs, Jesus

**The Writer:** One of the biggest mysteries in the entire New Testament is this: who wrote the book of Hebrews? It is believed the letter was written around AD 65, but there is no real agreement on who wrote it. Some experts believe the apostle Paul wrote this letter. Others believe the writer was Barnabas, who traveled with Paul on his first missionary journey. Others believe it was a man named Apollos, a Jewish preacher from Alexandria who had been taught by a married couple named Aquila and Priscilla (Acts 18:26).

## FUN BIBLE TRIVIA

Some Bible experts believe it is possible that a woman named Priscilla (who, along with her husband, Aquila, served the first-century church in Corinth and Ephesus) wrote the book of Hebrews. If that were true, Priscilla would be the only female author of a New Testament book.

## What You'll Find in the Book of Hebrews

**The writer of** Hebrews was probably addressing new Jewish Christians (that's why it's called "Hebrews") who might have been tempted to avoid persecution from other Jews and return to the system of sacrifices and other Old Testament–style ceremonies. The writer of Hebrews wanted his readers to understand that Jesus' sacrificial death eliminated the need for those kinds of observances.

In chapter 10, the writer to the Hebrews tells his readers that Jesus was far better than the Old Testament system of sacrifices. For one thing, the sacrificial system required people to make sacrifices once every year through a human priest to cover their sins. The perfect sacrifice of Jesus on the cross was a once-and-for-all sacrifice that allows each individual Christian to approach God without the help of a priest.

The writer of Hebrews encourages Jewish Christians to hold to their faith in Jesus, and also warns them not to neglect their faith (2:1–4), not to fall into unbelief (3:7–4:13), to continue to grow in their faith (5:11–6:20), and to endure persecution and other temptations to give up on their faith (10:32–39).

## POWER WORDS

*Let us fix our eyes on Jesus, the author and perfecter of our faith, who for the joy set before him endured the cross, scorning its shame, and sat down at the right hand of the throne of God.*

Hebrews 12:2 NIV

DISCOVER THE BIBLE

# James

**What It's About:** The apostle James writes that real Christian faith is shown in a believer's actions, especially in how he or she treats others.

**Important Characters/People:** James, teachers, church leaders

**The Writer:** The writer of this letter is believed to be James (also known as James the Just), the earthly brother of Jesus (see Matthew 13:55; Mark 6:3). The Bible tells us that James was not a Christian until after Jesus' resurrection (compare John 7:3–5 with Acts 1:14; 1 Corinthians 15:7; and Galatians 1:19). Once he became a Christian, he served as one of the leaders of the church in Jerusalem (see Galatians 2:9). The book of James is believed to be the oldest book of the New Testament, written as early as AD 45.

# What You'll Find in the Book of James

**Have you ever** heard the saying, "Don't just talk the talk—walk the walk"? That's the message behind the book of James, which encourages Christians to demonstrate their faith in a loving God by loving others through their actions. In a way, it's a more detailed explanation of these words of Jesus: " You should be a light for other people. Live so that they will see the good things you do and will praise your Father in heaven" (Matthew 5:16 NCV).

> **POWER WORDS**
> Come near to God, and God will come near to you.
> James 4:8 NCV

While Paul taught that Christians are saved by faith alone and not by the good things they do (see Romans 3:28), James teaches that good deeds should follow real faith. That's why he encourages all Christians to focus on living right, watching how they talk, and treating others as valuable in God's eyes—even during difficult times.

CHAPTER 8: LETTERS THAT BECAME BOOKS OF THE BIBLE

# 1 Peter

**What It's About:** When a believer suffers for Jesus, he or she should consider it a good thing.

**Important Characters/People:** Peter, church leaders

**The Writer:** The apostle Peter, with the assistance of Silvanus (5:12)

## What You'll Find in the Book of 1 Peter

**Peter wrote this** letter to Jewish Christians living all over the Roman Empire to encourage them and challenge them. They needed the encouragement, too, because Jewish Christians faced terrible treatment from the Jews and from the Romans.

Peter not only wrote to encourage Christians to endure the bad things that happened to them, but also to rejoice and to see it as a privilege to be mistreated because of their faith in Jesus.

Peter also encouraged Christians to put others ahead of themselves—just like Jesus did. When we do that, we not only become more like Jesus, but we will also receive rewards from God.

### POWER WORDS

*You are a chosen people. You are royal priests, a holy nation, God's very own possession. As a result, you can show others the goodness of God, for he called you out of the darkness into his wonderful light.*

1 Peter 2:9

# 2 Peter

**What It's About:** Peter warns believers to watch out for people who are spreading wrong teaching in the church.

**Important Characters/People:** Peter, prophets, false teachers

**The Writer:** The apostle Peter. He wrote this letter around AD 66 or 67, near the end of his life.

119

# What You'll Find in the Book of 2 Peter

**POWER WORDS**

*Because of his glory and excellence, he has given us great and precious promises. These are the promises that enable you to share his divine nature and escape the world's corruption caused by human desires.*
2 Peter 1:4

**Peter was troubled** because he knew that men were coming into the churches and spreading wrong teaching about the Christian faith. He encouraged Christians to grow strong in their faith and to focus on his teaching so that they would be able to tell when someone was trying to teach them wrong things.

Peter wrote that some of these false teachers even made fun of the truth that Jesus would return again (3:3–7). Instead of listening to them, he said, hold on to the promise of Jesus' return to earth; that truth will motivate us to live the way God wants us to live (3:14).

# 1 John

**What It's About:** Jesus was a real man—just as He was really God—and He set an example for Christians to follow in the way He loved others.

**Important Characters/People:** John

**The Writer:** The letters titled 1 John, 2 John, and 3 John don't mention who wrote them, but centuries of tradition hold that it was John, one of Jesus' 12 original disciples, who wrote these three letters around AD 92. John reminds his readers that he and the other disciples knew Jesus personally: "We saw him with our own eyes and touched him with our own hands" (1 John 1:1).

# What You'll Find in the Book of 1 John

**One of the** reasons John wrote this letter was to set believers straight about certain parts of the Christian faith. John knew that false teachers were trying to lead the Christians of that time away from the true Christian faith. The New Testament had not yet been put together into one book, so there was no single book that Christians could read in order to find out whether what they were being taught was true.

CHAPTER 8: LETTERS THAT BECAME BOOKS OF THE BIBLE

In the first two chapters of 1 John, the apostle writes about how a true Christian should live. He writes that people who claim to be Christians but don't live the way God wants them to live aren't really Christians at all (1:8). He also encourages Christians not to hide their sins but to confess them, because God is "faithful and just" to forgive those who confess their sins (1:9).

In chapters 3 and 4, John writes that God loves us so deeply, we should love Him in return and also love others the same way. John encourages his readers to love one another selflessly, even to the point of laying down their lives for one another if necessary (3:16–17).

John writes that "God is love" (4:8) and that those who really know God will love others as a result. On the other hand, those who don't love don't really know God at all. John says that when we love others, God lives within us (4:12).

In chapter 5, John writes that love and obedience to God are closely tied together and that we can approach God at any time, knowing that He hears us and will answer our prayers.

> **POWER WORDS**
>
> *See how very much our Father loves us, for he calls us his children, and that is what we are! But the people who belong to this world don't recognize that we are God's children because they don't know him.*
> 1 John 3:1

## 2 John

**What It's About:** The apostle John warns Christians to watch out for false teachers who don't believe in Jesus' physical life and ministry here on earth.

**Important Characters/People:** John, "the chosen lady and her children"

**The Writer:** The apostle John (see page 120)

# What You'll Find in the Book of 2 John

**The apostle John** addressed 2 John to "the chosen lady and to her children." That could have meant a woman of important position in the Ephesian church, or it could have meant the local church.

John wrote this letter to warn Christians against false teachers who taught that Jesus didn't physically rise from the dead, but rose only in a spiritual sense. John warned true believers to completely avoid people who taught that.

DISCOVER THE BIBLE

# 3 John

**What It's About:** True Christian leaders must be humble people who are more concerned about the welfare of others than they are for their own reputation or position.

**Important Characters/People:** John, Gaius, Diotrephes

**The Writer:** The apostle John (see page 120)

## What You'll Find in the Book of 3 John

**John's third epistle** was written to a Christian named Gaius (1:1). John wrote of Gaius as a man who demonstrated hospitality to traveling preachers who stopped off in his hometown. He also warns against the kind of leadership practiced by a man named Diotrephes, who was more interested in having power over people than he was in serving them.

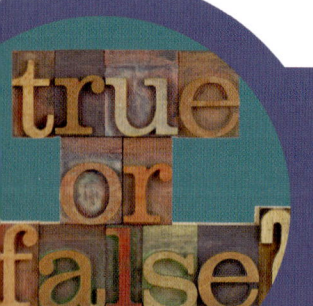

# Jude

**What It's About:** Jude warns Christians to watch out for those who try to spread wrong teaching.

**Important Characters/People:** Jude, Enoch

**The Writer:** The writer of the epistle of Jude identifies himself only as the "brother of James" (1:1). It's possible that Jude was the brother of James, who is identified as the brother of Jesus (see Matthew 13:55), but Jude does not identify himself as Jesus' brother.

## What You'll Find in the Book of Jude

**The book of** Jude was written between AD 60 and 80, and it deals with some of the same problems Peter addresses in his second letter. Jude wanted to warn Christians not to follow the example of false teachers in the church, who were leading people away from the faith; and complainers, who weren't living right.

# CHAPTER 9

## What's Ahead

### John's Vision of the Last Days (Revelation)

**By now, you** should have a pretty good idea of what the different books of the Bible are about, the key characters and events in each book, and what you can learn from reading each book.

Now we come to the last book of the Bible: Revelation. Though the Old Testament contains a lot of prophecy books, Revelation is the only New Testament book devoted to prophecy. Other New Testament books include *some* prophecy, but Revelation is the only one that is pretty much all prophecy.

Before you read on, there are some things about Revelation that you should know. First of all, this book has confused some of the most dedicated Bible scholars and Christian leaders, and it has led to some big disagreements. That's because the book uses lots of colorful imagery, and people disagree about what these symbols and pictures mean.

Revelation includes some very strange—and sometimes very scary—passages that can be taken many different ways. Some believe a lot of what we read in Revelation has already taken place and that the writer wrote the way he did in order to confuse Roman leaders who treated first-century Christians very badly. Other people believe that most of Revelation looks forward to events that haven't happened yet.

No matter what you believe about Revelation, it is a book that promises that things will turn out great for people who follow Jesus faithfully. And it also contains some practical words you can apply to your Christian life every day.

> **DID YOU KNOW. . . ?**
> The book of Revelation has also been called the Revelation of Jesus Christ, the Apocalypse of John, or simply the Apocalypse. The word *apocalypse* is sometimes used to describe worldwide destruction or a disaster, but it actually means an *unveiling* or *revealing*. That is why most people call this book Revelation.

DISCOVER THE BIBLE

# Revelation

**What It's About:** Jesus will return to earth and reward those who do right and punish those who do wrong. Revelation describes the final conflict between good and evil.

**Important Characters/People:** John, Jesus, the dragon (Satan), two beasts, the "messenger" angels

**The Writer:** The book of Revelation was written by John, one of Jesus' original 12 disciples, who also wrote the Gospel of John, 1 John, 2 John, and 3 John. He received the visions he writes about in this book while living on the island of Patmos, which is off the coast of Greece. The Roman government had sent him there as punishment for preaching the Good News of Jesus (see Revelation 1:9).

### POWER WORDS

*"I am the Alpha and the Omega—the beginning and the end," says the Lord God. "I am the one who is, who always was, and who is still to come—the Almighty One."*

Revelation 1:8

### WHO, WHAT, WHERE?

Revelation 1:9 says that John received the visions he wrote in the book while living as a prisoner on Patmos, an island located in the Aegean Sea, west of Asia Minor (now Turkey). Patmos covers about 13 square miles and is thought to have been an island prison of the Roman Empire. Today, Patmos is part of Greece.

## What You'll Find in the Book of Revelation

**Revelation starts by** telling readers what they are about to read: "The revelation of Jesus Christ, which God gave him to show his servants what must soon take place" (1:1 NIV). John then explains that he received the visions he writes about from an angel whom God had sent.

After greeting his readers, John writes that he heard a very loud voice instructing him to write down everything he was about to hear and see. Then he describes an amazing—and terrifying—vision of someone "like the Son of Man" (1:13). He was dressed in a long robe with a golden sash across his chest, and his head and hair were "white like wool, as white as snow," and his eyes were like "flames of fire" (1:14). His feet were like "polished bronze refined in a furnace" and his voice "thundered like mighty ocean waves" (1:15). He held seven stars in his hand and out of his mouth came a "sharp two-edged sword" (1:16). His face was like the shining sun (1:16).

CHAPTER 9: WHAT'S AHEAD

After hearing and seeing all this, John was so frightened that he fell on his face as if he were dead. But just then, the person in John's vision laid his hand on John's shoulder and told him not to be afraid, because, "I am the First and the Last. I am the living one. I died, but look—I am alive forever and ever! And I hold the keys of death and the grave" (1:17–18).

John knew who was talking to him. It was Jesus! This was the same Jesus with whom John had spent three years when Jesus was alive on earth. But even though it was the same Jesus, He looked and sounded different, because now He had been "glorified," which means he appeared in His heavenly form.

And He had a lot for John to think and write about!

## FUN BIBLE TRIVIA

The number seven appears many times in the book of Revelation (seven churches, seven horns, seven eyes, seven seals, seven trumpets, seven bowls). The number seven is important in Jewish tradition because it stands for God's perfection as He rested on the seventh day after He had finished creation. (Look it up in Genesis 2:2–3.)

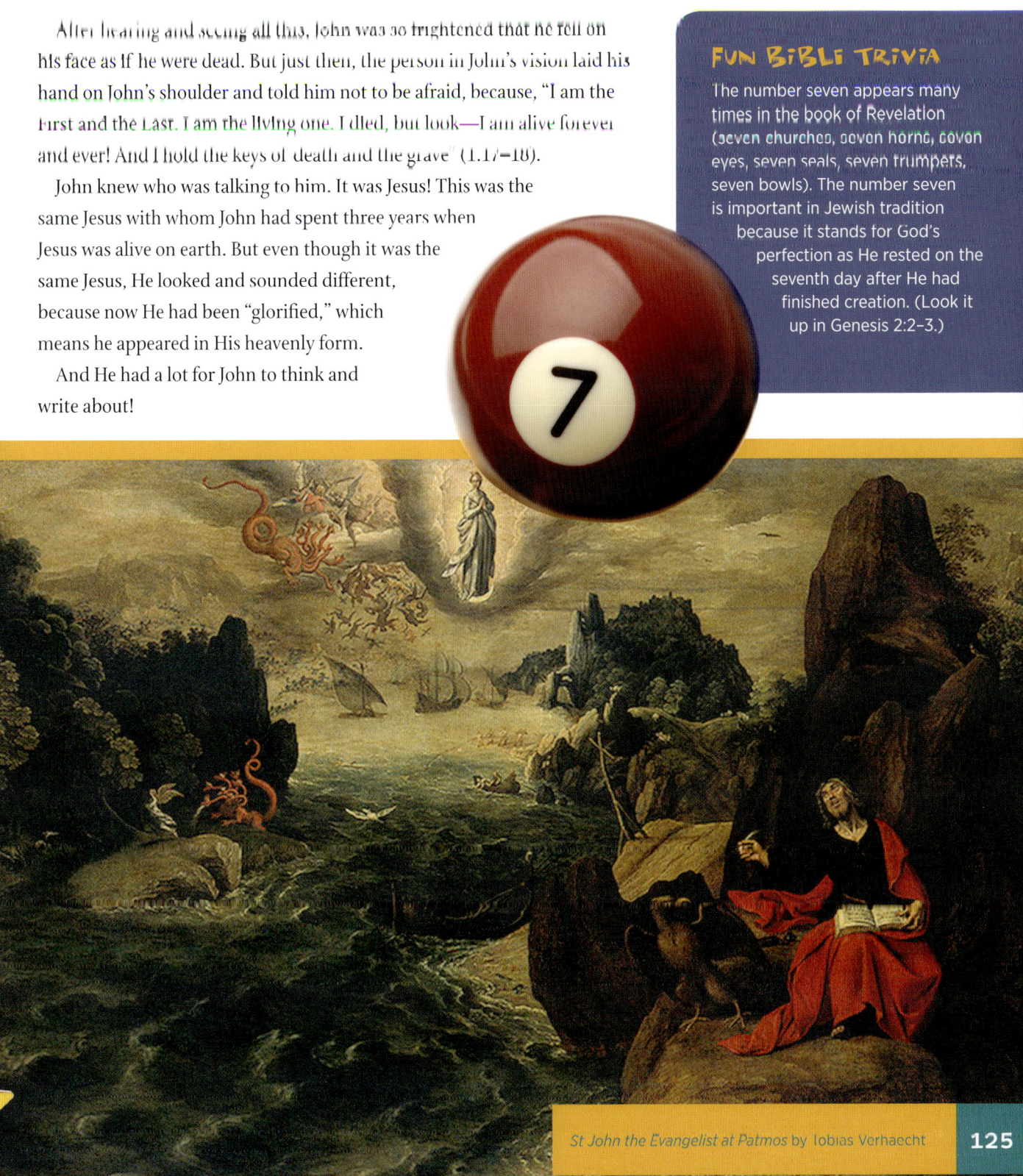

*St John the Evangelist at Patmos* by Tobias Verhaecht

DISCOVER THE BIBLE

## Seven Messages for Seven Churches

**Chapters 2 and 3** of Revelation are Jesus' own words for seven churches in Asia Minor, a place that is now part of the nation of Turkey. He encouraged some of the churches, but He challenged and criticized others.

Here is a quick look at what Jesus said to the seven churches.

1. **Ephesus (2:1–7):** Jesus praised this church for doing some good things, but He also called them to love Him and one another as they once had.
2. **Smyrna (2:8–11):** This church had little money or possessions, and they were spoken against by the outside world. But Jesus praised the church for their spiritual riches and encouraged them to "remain faithful even when facing death, [and] I will give you the crown of life" (verse 10).
3. **Pergamum (2:12–17):** Jesus gave this church high marks for remaining true to Him, even though they were treated terribly. But He also warned them to stop compromising when it came to the teaching they accepted.
4. **Thyatira (2:18–21):** Jesus noticed this church's love, faith, service, and endurance, but He warned them to get rid of the idolatry and sin that had made their way into the church.
5. **Sardis (3:1–6):** This church was spiritually asleep, and Jesus called them to wake up!
6. **Philadelphia (3:7–13):** Jesus praised this church for their faithfulness and perseverance—even though they had faced persecution from "Satan's synagogue," people who said they were Jews but were not.
7. **Laodicea (3:14–19):** Jesus reserved His toughest words for the Laodicean church because they were "'like lukewarm water, neither hot nor cold'" (3:16). Jesus called the Laodiceans to decide what they wanted to be and told them to "'be diligent and turn from your indifference'" (verse 19).

### WHAT'S IN IT FOR ME?

Revelation 3:14–22 contains Jesus' words to the church in Laodicea. They sound like harsh words for a church that had grown "lukewarm," but they can be an encouragement for you to make sure you approach your Christian faith with the kind of devotion and enthusiasm it deserves.

CHAPTER 9: WHAT'S AHEAD

In the last four verses of Revelation 3, Jesus calls the churches to a closer relationship with Him and promises them, "Those who are victorious will sit with me on my throne, just as I was victorious and sat with my Father on his throne" (3:21).

> ### POWER WORDS
> "Look! I stand at the door and knock. If you hear my voice and open the door, I will come in, and we will share a meal together as friends."
>
> Revelation 3:20

## John's Second Vision (Revelation 4–6)

**After hearing the** message to the seven churches, John received a second vision. This vision began with a door standing open in heaven and a voice—the same voice he had heard before—inviting him to see a throne room of God.

John saw quite a scene in the throne room. He saw a throne on which was seated a figure "as brilliant as gemstones" (4:3). This was Jesus, the Lamb of God, and His throne was surrounded by 24 more thrones, each with an "elder" sitting on it.

There were also four living creatures in the throne room, and each was covered with eyes from front to back. One looked like a lion, one like an ox, one like a human, and one like an eagle. Day after day, these creatures cried out, "Holy, holy, holy is the Lord God, the Almighty—the one who always was, who is, and who is still to come" (4:8).

In this vision, John also saw in the right hand of the one sitting on the main throne a scroll that was sealed with seven seals that no one on earth could open and read. John wept out loud because no one was worthy to open the scrolls, but one of the elders said, "Stop weeping! Look, the Lion of the tribe of Judah, the heir to David's throne, has won the victory. He is worthy to open the scroll and its seven seals" (5:5).

Then John saw a lamb that looked as if it had been slaughtered but was still standing. It had seven horns and seven eyes, and it was the one who could open the scroll. This was the Lamb of God—Jesus—and as He stepped forward to take the scroll, the 24 elders and four living creatures fell down before him and "sang a new song" (5:9).

127

DISCOVER THE BIBLE

# The Seven Seals (6:1–8:1)

**FUN BIBLE TRIVIA**

The first four seal judgments listed in Revelation 6 have been called the Four Horsemen of the Apocalypse, even though that title doesn't appear in the book of Revelation or anywhere else in the Bible.

**As John watched,** the Lamb of God broke the seven seals one by one. When he opened the first seal, a rider on a white horse appeared and "rode out to win many battles and gain the victory" (6:2). When the second seal was broken, another horse appeared—a red one this time. On its back was a rider who was given a sword and the authority to remove peace from the earth and bring war everywhere. When the third seal was broken, a rider on a black horse appeared, holding a pair of scales in his hand. The breaking of the fourth seal brought a rider on a green horse. The rider was called Death.

When the Lamb of God opened the fifth seal, John saw the souls of Christians who had been killed on account of their faith. These souls asked God when He would punish the people who had taken their lives. Then white robes were given to each of the martyred souls, and they were told to be patient.

The sixth seal brought a huge earthquake. The sun turned black, the moon was turned as red as blood, and what looked like stars fell to the earth. All the mountains and islands of the earth disappeared. It was such a terrible scene that people hid themselves in caves and rocks and hoped the mountains would fall on them so they could escape God's judgment. When the seventh seal was broken, John heard complete quiet in heaven for half an hour—which was just a moment of silence before the second set of God's judgments on the earth.

# CHAPTER 9: WHAT'S AHEAD

## The Seven Trumpets (8:2–11:19)

**In John's next** vision, he saw seven angels with trumpets. One at a time, the angels blew their trumpets, bringing a new judgment on the earth. The first trumpet brought "hail and fire mixed with blood" on the earth that burned up a third of the trees and grass.

When the second trumpet sounded, something that looked like a huge mountain of fire was thrown into the sea, killing one-third of all the things that lived there and destroying one-third of the ships. The third trumpet brought what looked like a flaming star out of the sky. When it landed, it polluted one-third of the fresh water on the earth, leading to the deaths of many people.

### Who, What, Where

Revelation 9:11 mentions a king who is "the angel from the bottomless pit," named Abaddon in Hebrew and Appolyon in Greek (which means "the Destroyer"). It's not certain who this king is, but some experts believe it is either the Antichrist or the devil himself.

When the fourth angel blew his trumpet, one-third of the sun and moon were struck, and one-third of the stars went dark. Then John looked up and saw an eagle crying, "Terror, terror, terror to all who belong to this world because of what will happen when the last three angels blow their trumpets" (8:13).

When the fifth trumpet was blown, John saw what looked like a star falling from the sky. The star "was given the key to the shaft of the bottomless pit" (9:1). When he opened it, smoke came out and darkened the sunlight and air with smoke. Then locustlike creatures with stingers came from the smoke and began attacking people who "did not have the seal of God on their foreheads" (9:4).

When the sixth trumpet sounded, an army of 200 million mounted troops wiped out one-third of humankind with "fire and smoke and burning sulfur" (9:18). Still, John wrote, "the people who did not die in these plagues still refused to repent of their evil deeds and turn to God" (9:20).

When the seventh angel blew his trumpet, John heard loud praise from heaven. The 24 elders fell on their faces and spoke praises to God, because "it is time to judge the dead and reward your servants" (11:18). There was lightning, thunder, a huge earthquake, and a hailstorm.

DISCOVER THE BIBLE

## The Arrival of the Antichrist (12–14)

**Chapters 12–14 of** Revelation cover the arrival of "the beast," which has also been called the Antichrist. In chapter 12, John first sees a vision of a large red dragon, with seven heads and 10 horns, who was kicked out of heaven. This was the devil himself.

Chapter 13 actually describes two beasts—one with seven heads and 10 horns that came out of the sea, and one with two horns and the voice of a dragon that came up out of the earth. This beast was allowed to do pretty much anything it wanted for 42 months (three and a half years)—including declaring war on Christians.

The second of these two beasts had all the power of the first beast and required all people to worship the first beast and to take a mark with the name of the beast or his number (666) on their right hand or forehead (see Revelation 13:16–18). Those who didn't receive this mark were not allowed to do any kind of business. This beast is later called "the false prophet."

> **FUN BIBLE TRIVIA**
>
> The book of Revelation doesn't use the name *Antichrist*, and neither did the apostle Paul when he wrote his second letter to the Thessalonians. He wrote that the Day of the Lord (Christ's return) would not come "until there is a great rebellion against God and the man of lawlessness is revealed" (2 Thessalonians 2:3).

CHAPTER 9: WHAT'S AHEAD

## The Seven Bowls (15:1–16:24)

**John's vision of** God's final judgment on the earth continues in Revelation 15. This time, seven angels carry the seven final plagues on the earth, which are called "bowls." Here are the seven "bowl judgments" listed in the book of Revelation:

1. Horrible sores break out on those who have received the "mark of the beast" (16:2).
2. The sea turns to blood (16:3).
3. Fresh water turns to blood (16:4–6).
4. People are scorched by intense heat (16:8–9).
5. Darkness and pain afflict humans (16:10–11).
6. The Euphrates River dries up, and armies gather for the Battle of Armageddon (16:12–16).
7. The earth is shaken with the worst earthquake ever—islands disappear and mountains are flattened, 75-pound hailstones fall from the sky, and a place called Babylon is divided into three sections (16:17–21).

> **WHO, WHAT, WHERE?**
> The apostle John uses the word *Armageddon* to describe the final conflict between God and the Antichrist. This word actually means "mount of Megiddo." Megiddo was an ancient city in northern Israel along the Kishon River. This is where many experts believe the final battle between good and evil will take place.

## The End of Babylon, the Beast, and the Devil Himself (17–20)

**After the seventh** and final bowl is poured out on the earth, a loud voice declares, "It is finished!" (16:17). Babylon had been split in three pieces, and the cities of many nations had been leveled. Every island had disappeared into the oceans and seas, and the mountains had been leveled.

> **WHO, WHAT, WHERE?**
> The book of Revelation tells us that a city called Babylon will be destroyed by God near the end of time. But what is the Babylon mentioned in this book? Many experts believe "Babylon" is a code word for the Roman Empire, which oppressed Christians at the time John wrote Revelation. Whatever Babylon is in Revelation, it seems to stand for everything evil and ungodly in the world.

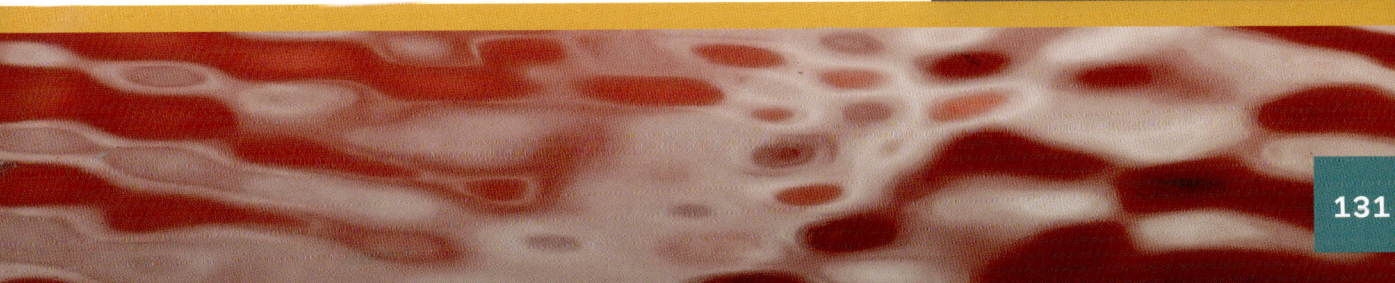

## DISCOVER THE BIBLE

### POWER WORDS

*Then I heard again what sounded like the shout of a vast crowd or the roar of mighty ocean waves or the crash of loud thunder: "Praise the LORD! For the Lord our God, the Almighty, reigns. Let us be glad and rejoice, and let us give honor to him. For the time has come for the wedding feast of the Lamb, and his bride has prepared herself."*
Revelation 19:6–7

### FUN BIBLE TRIVIA

The 1,000 years during which the devil will be tied up in chains and kept in the lake of fire while those who have served Christ will reign on earth is sometimes called the Millennium.

After this vision, one of the seven angels who poured the bowls of judgment out on the earth appeared to John and announced that Babylon would be destroyed and that the leaders of the nations would cry and grieve when they saw the city burning.

In heaven, on the other hand, there would be celebration that Babylon was finished (18:20).

Later in chapter 19, after John listened to an angel announcing the end of Babylon, he heard what sounded like a huge crowd in heaven praising God. As he continued to listen, he saw heaven open and a white horse with a rider named Faithful and True (19:11). The rider's eyes looked like blazing fire, and he had many crowns on his head and wore a robe dipped in blood. On his robe and on his thigh was the name "KING OF KINGS AND LORD OF LORDS" (19:11–16 NIV).

It was Jesus!

At the same time, the beast gathered his armies for the final battle against God and the armies of heaven. But it wasn't much of a battle. "Both the beast and his false prophet were thrown alive into the fiery lake of burning sulfur" (19:20), and their armies were destroyed.

Then John saw an angel come down from heaven and tie Satan up in chains and throw him into the same lake of fire, where he would stay for 1,000 years. During those 1,000 years, those who had died because of their

faith in Christ, as well as the people who hadn't worshipped the beast or taken his mark, "reigned with Christ" (20:4).

At the end of the 1,000 years, the devil was released from the lake of fire and immediately began deceiving people. He gathered an army and surrounded God's people, but he was then thrown into the lake of fire, where he, the beast, and the false prophet would stay forever.

With the devil taken care of for good, everyone who had died before was judged before a "great white throne" (20:11). They were judged for the things they had done when they were alive, and everyone whose name was not found in the Book of Life was thrown into the lake of fire.

## A Peek at Heaven (21–22)

**The book of** Revelation describes some pretty scary visions of judgment on the earth after the people had turned their backs on God. But we can be grateful that the story doesn't leave off there. As terrible as some of these events might seem, what you're about to read makes reading the scary stuff worth it.

The last two chapters of Revelation record John's visions of what is ahead for people who have put their faith in Jesus. Even though chapters 4–20 are very hard to understand, the remaining two chapters of Revelation spell things out so that they are easy to grasp.

These chapters cover how things will one day turn out for you and everyone else who knows Jesus. And it's something you can look forward to!

## In with the New

**After seeing the** devil and death being done away with, John saw in his vision "a new heaven and a new earth, for the old heaven and the old earth had disappeared" (21:1). The sea was also gone, and John saw a "new Jerusalem" coming down from heaven from God, "like a bride beautifully dressed for her husband" (21:2).

John then heard a voice saying, "Now the dwelling of God is with men, and he will live with them. They will be his people, and God himself will be with them and be their God. He will wipe every tear from their eyes. There will be no more death or mourning or crying or pain, for the old order of things has passed away" (21:3–4 NIV).

# DISCOVER THE BIBLE

## POWER WORDS

*"Look, I am coming soon, bringing my reward with me to repay all people according to their deeds. I am the Alpha and the Omega, the First and the Last, the Beginning and the End."*
Revelation 22:12–13

But that wasn't all. John heard that same voice saying, "I am making everything new! . . . Write this down, for what I tell you is trustworthy and true. . . . It is finished! I am the Alpha and the Omega—the Beginning and the End. To all who are thirsty I will give freely from the springs of the water of life. All who are victorious will inherit all these blessings, and I will be their God, and they will be my children" (21:5–7).

An angel then showed John the new Jerusalem, an amazing structure where there was no need for a sun or moon because God and His Son provided the light. A river flowed down the city's main street, and on each side of the street was the tree of life, which produced 12 different kinds of fruit—one for each month of the year.

It was from this place that God and His people would rule "forever and ever" (22:5). Nothing would be cursed any longer, and God's throne and Jesus' throne would be there, and His servants would worship Him.

The last 14 verses of Revelation—and of the Bible—include Jesus' promise, "I am coming soon" (22:7, 12, 20).

# CHAPTER 10

## Why You Should Read the Bible for Yourself... and How to Do It!

**Throughout this book,** you've seen little sidebars titled "What's in It for Me?" Those features were included to give you some ideas about what you can get out of certain portions of the Bible.

As you think about reading the Bible yourself, you might be wondering, *What's in it for me?* Lots of things! In fact, you should know that God wants you to desire to know the Bible more today than you did yesterday.

Here are five good reasons you should make reading the Bible a part of your life every day:

### 1. You can learn about God Himself. 
The Bible is filled to the brim with the things God has said, the things He has done, and the ways He has related to His people. When you read about those things, you get a good idea of what God is really like—what kind of person He is!

Do you want to know what makes God happy and what makes Him unhappy? Do you want to know what kinds of things people have done that make Him angry? Do you want to know what kind of love He has for you? There's no better way to learn these things than by opening up your Bible and reading what God has done and said.

> **POWER WORDS**
>
> *For the word of God is alive and powerful. It is sharper than the sharpest two-edged sword, cutting between soul and spirit, between joint and marrow. It exposes our innermost thoughts and desires.*
> Hebrews 4:12

### 2. You can learn what it takes to have a strong and growing relationship with God. 
When you became a Christian, God didn't just look down at you and say, "Great! Now you're the kind of person I want you to be! Now you can just wait around until it's time to go to heaven!"

## DISCOVER THE BIBLE

No, when you became a Christian, that was just the beginning of the work God wants to do in you. That's what the apostle Paul meant when he wrote, "I am certain that God, who began the good work within you, will continue his work until it is finally finished on the day when Christ Jesus returns" (Philippians 1:6).

Growing in your relationship with God doesn't just happen on its own, any more than your body grows on its own. Just as your body requires proper nourishment and exercise to grow bigger and stronger, your relationship with God requires nourishment and exercise to grow bigger and stronger. And where do you get that nourishment? From the pages of your Bible!

### 3. You can learn how to be more and more like Jesus.
The Bible teaches that our goal as Christians is to become more and more like Jesus every day. That means you should be more like Him tomorrow than you were today—and a lot more like Him next year than you are right now.

Jesus is your perfect example of how to live, how to think, how to love God, and how to treat other people. And the more you're like Him in every way, the more you please God, and the more you let people around you see how amazing He really is!

Okay, so now that you know that God wants you to be more and more like Jesus every day, the question is, how can you learn what Jesus was like? By reading the Bible! You can see what Jesus was really like—how He thought, prayed, lived, and cared for others—by reading the books of the Bible called the Gospels. Remember where they are? If not, turn back in this book to chapter 6 for a quick reminder.

But you don't need to stop at just the Gospels. Remember, Jesus was God in human form, and everything God the Father says, does, and thinks, Jesus does, says, and thinks right along with Him. So you can learn to be more like Jesus by reading from the entire Bible!

### 4. You can learn how God wants you to live.
Someone once said that being a Christian isn't about following a bunch of rules; it's about having a real, personal relationship with God through Jesus Christ.

---

**POWER WORDS**

*All Scripture is inspired by God and is useful to teach us what is true and to make us realize what is wrong in our lives. It corrects us when we are wrong and teaches us to do what is right.*

2 Timothy 3:16

How true that is!

At the same time, though, the Bible includes a lot of really important commands, encouragements, promises, and guidelines for living the Christian life. So if you want to know how God wants you to live, go straight to the source for His instructions: the Bible!

You almost can't open your Bible without finding some of God's commands, encouragements, promises, and guidelines for life. So when you read your Bible, pay close attention to things God might want you to focus on. Hint: Pay *really* close attention when you're reading books like Proverbs, the Gospels, and the New Testament epistles (Romans through Jude).

## 5. You can learn how God wants you to treat other people.

More than anything, the Bible is about how to have a relationship with God. But it also has a lot to say about how to treat other people, especially other Christians.

If there is one statement that tells us how we are to treat others, it is Jesus' words to His disciples just before His death on the cross: "A new command I give you: Love one another" (John 13:34 NIV). The apostle John, who recorded those words from Jesus, also wrote, "Dear friends, let us love one another, for love comes from God" (1 John 4:7 NIV).

But what does it mean for us to love one another? Should we just have warm, fuzzy feelings for other people? Should we just tell people that we love them and let that be good enough? No! The Bible teaches that we show our love through our words and also through our actions.

You can find great guidelines for how to treat people with God's love in many places in the Bible. If you want a good place to start, read Jesus' teaching—and pay close attention to the Sermon on the Mount (Matthew 5–7). You can also find some great guidelines for how to treat others by reading the book of Proverbs and the New Testament epistles.

Show love for one another with your actions.

# Now for the "Hows" of Bible Reading and Study

**Okay, now you** have a pretty good idea of *why* you should read the Bible. But if you're like most Christians, you are probably wondering *how* to do it. If you're not sure about the best way to approach reading and studying the Bible, don't feel bad. Just realize that there are a lot of really good ways to read the Bible so that you can get the very most out of it.

First is the most obvious way: reading it cover to cover, starting with Genesis 1 and ending with Revelation 22. The best thing about reading the Bible from beginning to end is that you get a good idea of the order in which things happened (keeping in mind that the Old Testament prophecy books were written during different times in Israel's history).

It's a good idea for any Christian to read the Bible all the way through at least once. And it's not as hard as you might think, especially since there are so many prepared schedules you can use to get it done in one year. (See appendix A for a one-year Bible-reading schedule.)

But reading through the Bible in a year—or in less time if you're a fast reader—is only the beginning. And truthfully, if you want to get the most out of your Bible reading, it's a good idea to do it in ways other than just cover to cover.

# CHAPTER 10: WHY YOU SHOULD READ THE BIBLE FOR YOURSELF. . .AND HOW YOU DO IT!

## Don't Just Read. . . . Study!

**Have you ever** read something—part of one of your school textbooks, for example—only to forget what you read five minutes later? Some people have a talent for remembering everything they read, but most of us need to put in some extra effort to remember what we read.

That extra effort is called studying. Studying means not just to read something, but to read it over again, think about what you've read, and try to learn as much as you can from what you've read.

The Bible is a great book to study—by yourself, with your family, with your friends. And just as there are all kinds of settings to study the Bible in, there are also all kinds of ways to do it.

Here are some great ways to study your Bible:

## Studying in a Certain Book

**One of the** things you've learned in reading this book—we hope—is that each book of the Bible has its own writer, its own story, its own background, and its own topics and ideas. Obviously, there's no better way to find out those things about a certain book of the Bible than by reading and studying it yourself.

That's where a book like this one can come in really handy. When you decide you want to read and study a book of the Bible, you can look up *that* book in *this* book to learn the basics.

For example, if you want to read and study the Gospel of Matthew, you can take a look at what this book has to tell you about that particular Gospel. You'll learn that it was written by a man named Matthew, that it was originally written to Jewish people, and that it has a lot to say about how Jesus fulfilled Old Testament prophecies about the coming Messiah.

You'll be amazed just how much knowing things like that will help you as you prepare to read and study a certain book of the Bible. Go ahead and try it!

## Studying a Certain Word

**Are there words** from the Bible you have heard but don't know exactly what they mean—at least what they mean in the Bible? Do you know what the word *grace* means? How about *mercy* or *pardon*? You can learn what the Bible means when it uses those words when you read and study the Bible using key words that appear in the different books.

# DISCOVER THE BIBLE

To do this kind of study, all you need is your Bible and a concordance, a reference book that lists the different words used in the Bible and tells you where you can find them. If you don't have a concordance, then you can use one of several online concordances available on the Internet.

When you study the Bible this way, try using different forms of different words—for example, when you want to study God's forgiveness, take the time to look up the words *forgive, forgiving,* and *forgiven.* You can also look up different words that mean the same thing (these words are called synonyms). That way, you'll get a better idea of what those words mean in the Bible.

Some good words to start with are *love, grace, mercy, pardon,* and *forgiveness*—simply because these words are so much a part of God's character.

## What's in it For Me?

If you want to get the absolute most you can out of your Bible study, it's a good idea to have at least some of these tools to help you out:

**Bible**: This might seem too obvious to mention, but which Bible you choose will go a long way in determining how much you learn in your Bible study. Choose a translation that is easy for you to understand, and you'll get a lot more out of your Bible study.

**Dictionary**: A good dictionary is always handy to have when you're studying anything, including the Bible. When you see a word you don't know, you can look it up in your dictionary to see what it means.

**Bible Dictionary**: There are a lot of good Bible dictionaries out there to help you with your study. You can even find good ones on the Internet. A Bible dictionary will explain what certain words and ideas mean in the Bible.

**Concordance**: Remember, this is a book made up of an alphabetical list of all Bible words.

**Bible Commentary**: There are a lot of great Bible commentaries written by people who know the Bible cover to cover. A Bible commentary can help you gain insights when you study. You can find good Bible commentaries online, at your library, or at the local bookstore.

**Bible Atlas**: An atlas is a book of maps that will help you understand where the Bible stories you read took place. It can also help you to understand more about the stories and other passages you read.

**Pencil and Paper**: Bible study time is a good time to take some notes!

# CHAPTER 10: WHY YOU SHOULD READ THE BIBLE FOR YOURSELF. . .AND HOW YOU DO IT!

## Studying a Certain Subject

**If your teacher** were to give you an assignment to write a report about a certain animal—let's say a giraffe—how would you research giraffes so that you could write a good report? You probably wouldn't check out a library book about animals that live in Africa and start reading it cover to cover, would you? More than likely, you'd check out that same book and go directly to the section about giraffes. That would save you a lot of time and also allow you to learn more about giraffes because you had spent some time learning all you could about them.

You can study your Bible the same way. Let's say you want to study what the Bible has to say about the subject of God's forgiveness. You'd look up verses and passages in both the Old Testament and the New Testament that had to do with God's forgiveness. Then you would focus on what those verses and passages said, how they were the same or different, and how they applied to you.

By the time you were done doing this kind of study, you'd have a pretty good idea of what God says about any subject you chose.

## Studying a Certain Passage (Section)

**The Bible is** filled with some amazing sections—sometimes called passages—with some great lessons for you today. Another great way to read and study the Bible is to concentrate on one of those sections and see what God is saying to you through it.

As you study a passage of the Bible, pay close attention to the things people do and say, as well as what happened as a result. Don't forget to notice how God responds to the things that people do and say.

There are literally hundreds of great Bible passages to study and learn from. Here are just a few to help you get started with your own study of the Bible:

Genesis 1–2—The creation of the universe, the earth, and humans
Genesis 6:9–8:22—Noah and the flood
Joshua 1—God's instructions and encouragement for Joshua
1 Samuel 17:12–54—David's battle with the giant Goliath
Psalm 1—The blessed man
Daniel 6—The prophet Daniel in the lions' den
Luke 2:1–20—The birth of Jesus

Matthew 5–7—Jesus' Sermon on the Mount
Acts 2—The believers in Jerusalem receive the Holy Spirit
1 Corinthians 13—The "love chapter"
Hebrews 11—Great biblical examples of faith

## Studying Certain People, Places, and Things

### Who, What, Where?

Do you want a good list to start with as you study the lives of important people in the Bible? Try these names first: Adam and Eve, Noah, Abraham, Joseph, Moses, Joshua, David, Solomon, Jesus (of course!), Peter, the apostle John, and the apostle Paul. Of course, there are hundreds of other people you can study, but this list gives you a good place to start.

**The Bible has** many examples of how God deals with people—with His own people as well as with people who do not know Him. Another great way to study the Bible is to focus on the people, places, and events of the Bible.

Who are some of the people from the Bible you want to know more about? Adam and Eve? Moses? Joshua? David? Jesus and His disciples? The apostle Paul? Take the time to read all you can about these people (it never hurts to use a Bible dictionary or encyclopedia to help you along), and as you read, pay close attention to their lives—the things they did right, the things they did wrong, and the way God responded to them.

When you focus your attention on a personality from the Bible and learn all you can about him or her, you will find that person's story is filled with great lessons for your own life.

One quick note: When you start a study on a certain person in the Bible, make sure you aren't reading about two or more different people who went by the same name. That's easier to do than you might think. There are 28 men in the Bible named Azariah, 27 named Zechariah, and 25 named Shemaiah. Altogether, there are 23 names connected with 10 or more people.

As for studying places and things, you can apply the same steps you would use if you were studying a person.

# Other Things You Can Do with the Bible

**Of course, reading** and studying your Bible are things God wants you to do. But did you know you can take your reading and studying to another level—or two or three?

As this book draws to a finish, we want you to think about some of the things you can use the Bible for. Some of them might surprise you!

## Memorize Bible Verses

**Have you ever** met someone who seemed to have the ability to quote Bible verses off the top of his or her head? Or maybe you've noticed the pastor or teachers at your church can quote verses without looking them up?

Those things don't just happen. Usually, people who can quote Bible passages have spent time memorizing some of the more important verses. It's not as hard as it sounds. All it takes is a little repetition, a little time, and some effort.

What are some of the benefits of memorizing Bible verses? Suppose you had a friend who wanted to know more about your Christian faith. Of course you can tell that person what God has done for you, but when you can remember some important passages from the Bible, you can better explain what the Bible says about becoming a Christian.

> **POWER WORDS**
>
> *I have hidden your word in my heart, that I might not sin against you.*
>
> Psalm 119:11

## DISCOVER THE BIBLE

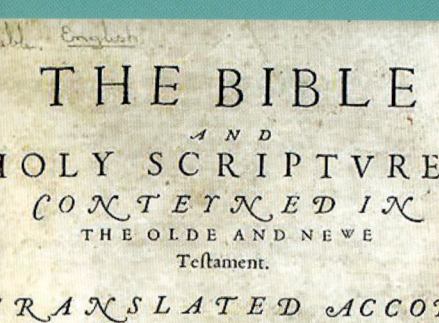

One of the best ways to memorize Bible verses is to simply read them over and over until they are recorded in your memory. And it really helps when you follow these basic Bible memorization steps:

- **Pick out a Bible version you like and can most easily understand.**
- **Pick out the verse or verses you want to memorize.**
- **Don't try to memorize too much at once.**
- **Write the verse or verses down. Use flash cards if that helps.**
- **Work with a friend or family member.**

One last thing: It's good to memorize the words of different Bible verses, but it's also really helpful to memorize where they are in the Bible. That means you should also memorize the book, the chapter, and the verse where you found the words you have memorized.

## Take It Personally!

**Have you ever** thought of the words recorded in your Bible as God's personal message to you? Well, you can, because that's exactly what they are! God made sure that every important word, thought, promise, command, and warning made it into the pages of your Bible, and He did that just for you.

One of the best ways to really personalize the Bible is to read a particular passage or verse and then write it down using words like *I* and *me* when the Bible says "you." For example, you can write down Philippians 4:19, which says, "My God shall supply all your need according to His riches in glory by Christ Jesus" (NKJV), like this:

> **My God shall supply all MY needs according to His riches in glory by Christ Jesus!**

When you read and study the Bible that way, you'll understand more and more every day that the Bible is a book written just for you.

And you'll also see how cool a book it really is.

### DID YOU KNOW...?
In 1560, the Geneva Bible was printed. It was the first English Bible with a feature that makes Bible memorization easier today: chapter and verse divisions. Three years before that, an Englishman named William Whittingham produced the first English-language New Testament with verse divisions.

# APPENDIX A

## Through the Bible in a Year

### A 365-Day Bible-Reading Schedule

Start your own Bible adventure—read through the whole Bible in a year. It'll only take you about 20 minutes a day!

|  | | | |
|---|---|---|---|
| Day 1 | Genesis 1–2 | Matthew 1 | Psalm 1 |
| Day 2 | Genesis 3–4 | Matthew 2 | Psalm 2 |
| Day 3 | Genesis 5–7 | Matthew 3 | Psalm 3 |
| Day 4 | Genesis 8–10 | Matthew 4 | Psalm 4 |
| Day 5 | Genesis 11–13 | Matthew 5:1–20 | Psalm 5 |
| Day 6 | Genesis 14–16 | Matthew 5:21–48 | Psalm 6 |
| Day 7 | Genesis 17–18 | Matthew 6:1–18 | Psalm 7 |
| Day 8 | Genesis 19–20 | Matthew 6:19–34 | Psalm 8 |
| Day 9 | Genesis 21–23 | Matthew 7:1–11 | Psalm 9:1–8 |
| Day 10 | Genesis 24 | Matthew 7:12–29 | Psalm 9:9–20 |
| Day 11 | Genesis 25–26 | Matthew 8:1–17 | Psalm 10:1–11 |
| Day 12 | Genesis 27:1–28:9 | Matthew 8:18–34 | Psalm 10:12–18 |
| Day 13 | Genesis 28:10–29:35 | Matthew 9 | Psalm 11 |
| Day 14 | Genesis 30:1–31:21 | Matthew 10:1–15 | Psalm 12 |
| Day 15 | Genesis 31:22–32:21 | Matthew 10:16–36 | Psalm 13 |
| Day 16 | Genesis 32:22–34:31 | Matthew 10:37–11:6 | Psalm 14 |
| Day 17 | Genesis 35–36 | Matthew 11:7–24 | Psalm 15 |
| Day 18 | Genesis 37–38 | Matthew 11:25–30 | Psalm 16 |
| Day 19 | Genesis 39–40 | Matthew 12:1–29 | Psalm 17 |
| Day 20 | Genesis 41 | Matthew 12:30–50 | Psalm 18:1–15 |
| Day 21 | Genesis 42–43 | Matthew 13:1–9 | Psalm 18:16–29 |
| Day 22 | Genesis 44–45 | Matthew 13:10–23 | Psalm 18:30–50 |

| | | | |
|---|---|---|---|
| Day 23 | Genesis 46:1–47:26 | Matthew 13:24–43 | Psalm 19 |
| Day 24 | Genesis 47:27–49:28 | Matthew 13:44–58 | Psalm 20 |
| Day 25 | Genesis 49:29–Exodus 1:22 | Matthew 14 | Psalm 21 |
| Day 26 | Exodus 2–3 | Matthew 15:1–28 | Psalm 22:1–21 |
| Day 27 | Exodus 4:1–5:21 | Matthew 15:29–16:12 | Psalm 22:22–31 |
| Day 28 | Exodus 5:22–7:24 | Matthew 16:13–28 | Psalm 23 |
| Day 29 | Exodus 7:25–9:35 | Matthew 17:1–9 | Psalm 24 |
| Day 30 | Exodus 10–11 | Matthew 17:10–27 | Psalm 25 |
| Day 31 | Exodus 12 | Matthew 18:1–20 | Psalm 26 |
| Day 32 | Exodus 13–14 | Matthew 18:21–35 | Psalm 27 |
| Day 33 | Exodus 15–16 | Matthew 19:1–15 | Psalm 28 |
| Day 34 | Exodus 17–19 | Matthew 19:16–30 | Psalm 29 |
| Day 35 | Exodus 20–21 | Matthew 20:1–19 | Psalm 30 |
| Day 36 | Exodus 22–23 | Matthew 20:20–34 | Psalm 31:1–8 |
| Day 37 | Exodus 24–25 | Matthew 21:1–27 | Psalm 31:9–18 |
| Day 38 | Exodus 26–27 | Matthew 21:28–46 | Psalm 31:19–24 |
| Day 39 | Exodus 28 | Matthew 22 | Psalm 32 |
| Day 40 | Exodus 29 | Matthew 23:1–36 | Psalm 33:1–12 |
| Day 41 | Exodus 30–31 | Matthew 23:37–24:28 | Psalm 33:13–22 |
| Day 42 | Exodus 32–33 | Matthew 24:29–51 | Psalm 34:1–7 |
| Day 43 | Exodus 34:1–35:29 | Matthew 25:1–13 | Psalm 34:8–22 |
| Day 44 | Exodus 35:30–37:29 | Matthew 25:14–30 | Psalm 35:1–8 |
| Day 45 | Exodus 38–39 | Matthew 25:31–46 | Psalm 35:9–17 |
| Day 46 | Exodus 40 | Matthew 26:1–35 | Psalm 35:18–28 |
| Day 47 | Leviticus 1–3 | Matthew 26:36–68 | Psalm 36:1–6 |
| Day 48 | Leviticus 4:1–5:13 | Matthew 26:69–27:26 | Psalm 36:7–12 |
| Day 49 | Leviticus 5:14–7:21 | Matthew 27:27–50 | Psalm 37:1–6 |
| Day 50 | Leviticus 7:22–8:36 | Matthew 27:51–66 | Psalm 37:7–26 |
| Day 51 | Leviticus 9–10 | Matthew 28 | Psalm 37:27–40 |
| Day 52 | Leviticus 11–12 | Mark 1:1–28 | Psalm 38 |
| Day 53 | Leviticus 13 | Mark 1:29–39 | Psalm 39 |
| Day 54 | Leviticus 14 | Mark 1:40–2:12 | Psalm 40:1–8 |
| Day 55 | Leviticus 15 | Mark 2:13–3:35 | Psalm 40:9–17 |
| Day 56 | Leviticus 16–17 | Mark 4:1–20 | Psalm 41:1–4 |
| Day 57 | Leviticus 18–19 | Mark 4:21–41 | Psalm 41:5–13 |

# APPENDIX A

| | | | |
|---|---|---|---|
| Day 58 | Leviticus 20 | Mark 5 | Psalm 42–43 |
| Day 59 | Leviticus 21–22 | Mark 6:1–13 | Psalm 44 |
| Day 60 | Leviticus 23–24 | Mark 6:14–29 | Psalm 45:1–5 |
| Day 61 | Leviticus 25 | Mark 6:30–56 | Psalm 45:6–12 |
| Day 62 | Leviticus 26 | Mark 7 | Psalm 45:13–17 |
| Day 63 | Leviticus 27 | Mark 8 | Psalm 46 |
| Day 64 | Numbers 1–2 | Mark 9:1–13 | Psalm 47 |
| Day 65 | Numbers 3 | Mark 9:14–50 | Psalm 48:1–8 |
| Day 66 | Numbers 4 | Mark 10:1–34 | Psalm 48:9–14 |
| Day 67 | Numbers 5:1–6:21 | Mark 10:35–52 | Psalm 49:1–9 |
| Day 68 | Numbers 6:22–7:47 | Mark 11 | Psalm 49:10–20 |
| Day 69 | Numbers 7:48–8:4 | Mark 12:1–27 | Psalm 50:1–15 |
| Day 70 | Numbers 8:5–9:23 | Mark 12:28–44 | Psalm 50:16–23 |
| Day 71 | Numbers 10–11 | Mark 13:1–8 | Psalm 51:1–9 |
| Day 72 | Numbers 12–13 | Mark 13:9–37 | Psalm 51:10–19 |
| Day 73 | Numbers 14 | Mark 14:1–31 | Psalm 52 |
| Day 74 | Numbers 15 | Mark 14:32–72 | Psalm 53 |
| Day 75 | Numbers 16 | Mark 15:1–32 | Psalm 54 |
| Day 76 | Numbers 17–18 | Mark 15:33–47 | Psalm 55 |
| Day 77 | Numbers 19–20 | Mark 16 | Psalm 56:1–7 |
| Day 78 | Numbers 21:1–22:20 | Luke 1:1–25 | Psalm 56:8–13 |
| Day 79 | Numbers 22:21–23:30 | Luke 1:26–56 | Psalm 57 |
| Day 80 | Numbers 24–25 | Luke 1:57–2:20 | Psalm 58 |
| Day 81 | Numbers 26:1–27:11 | Luke 2:21–38 | Psalm 59:1–8 |
| Day 82 | Numbers 27:12–29:11 | Luke 2:39–52 | Psalm 59:9–17 |
| Day 83 | Numbers 29:12–30:16 | Luke 3 | Psalm 60:1–5 |
| Day 84 | Numbers 31 | Luke 4 | Psalm 60:6–12 |
| Day 85 | Numbers 32–33 | Luke 5:1–16 | Psalm 61 |
| Day 86 | Numbers 34–36 | Luke 5:17–32 | Psalm 62:1–6 |
| Day 87 | Deuteronomy 1:1–2:25 | Luke 5:33–6:11 | Psalm 62:7–12 |
| Day 88 | Deuteronomy 2:26–4:14 | Luke 6:12–35 | Psalm 63:1–5 |
| Day 89 | Deuteronomy 4:15–5:22 | Luke 6:36–49 | Psalm 63:6–11 |
| Day 90 | Deuteronomy 5:23–7:26 | Luke 7:1–17 | Psalm 64:1–5 |
| Day 91 | Deuteronomy 8–9 | Luke 7:18–35 | Psalm 64:6–10 |
| Day 92 | Deuteronomy 10–11 | Luke 7:36–8:3 | Psalm 65:1–8 |

| | | | |
|---|---|---|---|
| Day 93 | Deuteronomy 12–13 | Luke 8:4–21 | Psalm 65:9–13 |
| Day 94 | Deuteronomy 14:1–16:8 | Luke 8:22–39 | Psalm 66:1–7 |
| Day 95 | Deuteronomy 16:9–18:22 | Luke 8:40–56 | Psalm 66:8–15 |
| Day 96 | Deuteronomy 19:1–21:9 | Luke 9:1–22 | Psalm 66:16–20 |
| Day 97 | Deuteronomy 21:10–23:8 | Luke 9:23–42 | Psalm 67 |
| Day 98 | Deuteronomy 23:9–25:19 | Luke 9:43–62 | Psalm 68:1–6 |
| Day 99 | Deuteronomy 26:1–28:14 | Luke 10:1–20 | Psalm 68:7–14 |
| Day 100 | Deuteronomy 28:15–68 | Luke 10:21–37 | Psalm 68:15–19 |
| Day 101 | Deuteronomy 29–30 | Luke 10:38–11:23 | Psalm 68:20–27 |
| Day 102 | Deuteronomy 31:1–32:22 | Luke 11:24–36 | Psalm 68:28–35 |
| Day 103 | Deuteronomy 32:23–33:29 | Luke 11:37–54 | Psalm 69:1–9 |
| Day 104 | Deuteronomy 34–Joshua 2 | Luke 12:1–15 | Psalm 69:10–17 |
| Day 105 | Joshua 3:1–5:12 | Luke 12:16–40 | Psalm 69:18–28 |
| Day 106 | Joshua 5:13–7:26 | Luke 12:41–48 | Psalm 69:29–36 |
| Day 107 | Joshua 8–9 | Luke 12:49–59 | Psalm 70 |
| Day 108 | Joshua 10:1–11:15 | Luke 13:1–21 | Psalm 71:1–6 |
| Day 109 | Joshua 11:16–13:33 | Luke 13:22–35 | Psalm 71:7–16 |
| Day 110 | Joshua 14–16 | Luke 14:1–15 | Psalm 71:17–21 |
| Day 111 | Joshua 17:1–19:16 | Luke 14:16–35 | Psalm 71:22–24 |
| Day 112 | Joshua 19:17–21:42 | Luke 15:1–10 | Psalm 72:1–11 |
| Day 113 | Joshua 21:43–22:34 | Luke 15:11–32 | Psalm 72:12–20 |
| Day 114 | Joshua 23–24 | Luke 16:1–18 | Psalm 73:1–9 |
| Day 115 | Judges 1–2 | Luke 16:19–17:10 | Psalm 73:10–20 |
| Day 116 | Judges 3–4 | Luke 17:11–37 | Psalm 73:21–28 |
| Day 117 | Judges 5:1–6:24 | Luke 18:1–17 | Psalm 74:1–3 |
| Day 118 | Judges 6:25–7:25 | Luke 18:18–43 | Psalm 74:4–11 |
| Day 119 | Judges 8:1–9:23 | Luke 19:1–28 | Psalm 74:12–17 |
| Day 120 | Judges 9:24–10:18 | Luke 19:29–48 | Psalm 74:18–23 |
| Day 121 | Judges 11:1–12:7 | Luke 20:1–26 | Psalm 75:1–7 |
| Day 122 | Judges 12:8–14:20 | Luke 20:27–47 | Psalm 75:8–10 |
| Day 123 | Judges 15–16 | Luke 21:1–19 | Psalm 76:1–7 |
| Day 124 | Judges 17–18 | Luke 21:20–22:6 | Psalm 76:8–12 |
| Day 125 | Judges 19:1–20:23 | Luke 22:7–30 | Psalm 77:1–11 |
| Day 126 | Judges 20:24–21:25 | Luke 22:31–54 | Psalm 77:12–20 |
| Day 127 | Ruth 1–2 | Luke 22:55–23:25 | Psalm 78:1–4 |

# APPENDIX A

| | | | |
|---|---|---|---|
| Day 128 | Ruth 3–4 | Luke 23:26–24:12 | Psalm 78:5–8 |
| Day 129 | 1 Samuel 1:1–2:21 | Luke 24:13–53 | Psalm 78:9–16 |
| Day 130 | 1 Samuel 2:22–4:22 | John 1:1–28 | Psalm 78:17–24 |
| Day 131 | 1 Samuel 5–7 | John 1:29–51 | Psalm 78:25–33 |
| Day 132 | 1 Samuel 8:1–9:26 | John 2 | Psalm 78:34–41 |
| Day 133 | 1 Samuel 9:27–11:15 | John 3:1–22 | Psalm 78:42–55 |
| Day 134 | 1 Samuel 12–13 | John 3:23–4:10 | Psalm 78:56–66 |
| Day 135 | 1 Samuel 14 | John 4:11–38 | Psalm 78:67–72 |
| Day 136 | 1 Samuel 15–16 | John 4:39–54 | Psalm 79:1–7 |
| Day 137 | 1 Samuel 17 | John 5:1–24 | Psalm 79:8–13 |
| Day 138 | 1 Samuel 18–19 | John 5:25–47 | Psalm 80:1–7 |
| Day 139 | 1 Samuel 20–21 | John 6:1–21 | Psalm 80:8–19 |
| Day 140 | 1 Samuel 22–23 | John 6:22–42 | Psalm 81:1–10 |
| Day 141 | 1 Samuel 24:1–25:31 | John 6:43–71 | Psalm 81:11–16 |
| Day 142 | 1 Samuel 25:32–27:12 | John 7:1–24 | Psalm 82 |
| Day 143 | 1 Samuel 28–29 | John 7:25–8:11 | Psalm 83 |
| Day 144 | 1 Samuel 30–31 | John 8:12–47 | Psalm 84:1–4 |
| Day 145 | 2 Samuel 1–2 | John 8:48–9:12 | Psalm 84:5–12 |
| Day 146 | 2 Samuel 3–4 | John 9:13–34 | Psalm 85:1–7 |
| Day 147 | 2 Samuel 5:1–7:17 | John 9:35–10:10 | Psalm 85:8–13 |
| Day 148 | 2 Samuel 7:18–10:19 | John 10:11–30 | Psalm 86:1–10 |
| Day 149 | 2 Samuel 11:1–12:25 | John 10:31–11:16 | Psalm 86:11–17 |
| Day 150 | 2 Samuel 12:26–13:39 | John 11:17–54 | Psalm 87 |
| Day 151 | 2 Samuel 14:1–15:12 | John 11:55–12:19 | Psalm 88:1–9 |
| Day 152 | 2 Samuel 15:13–16:23 | John 12:20–43 | Psalm 88:10–18 |
| Day 153 | 2 Samuel 17:1–18:18 | John 12:44–13:20 | Psalm 89:1–6 |
| Day 154 | 2 Samuel 18:19–19:39 | John 13:21–38 | Psalm 89:7–13 |
| Day 155 | 2 Samuel 19:40–21:22 | John 14:1–17 | Psalm 89:14–18 |
| Day 156 | 2 Samuel 22:1–23:7 | John 14:18–15:27 | Psalm 89:19–29 |
| Day 157 | 2 Samuel 23:8–24:25 | John 16:1–22 | Psalm 89:30–37 |
| Day 158 | 1 Kings 1 | John 16:23–17:5 | Psalm 89:38–52 |
| Day 159 | 1 Kings 2 | John 17:6–26 | Psalm 90:1–12 |
| Day 160 | 1 Kings 3–4 | John 18:1–27 | Psalm 90:13–17 |
| Day 161 | 1 Kings 5–6 | John 18:28–19:5 | Psalm 91:1–10 |
| Day 162 | 1 Kings 7 | John 19:6–25a | Psalm 91:11–16 |

## DISCOVER THE BIBLE

| Day | Old Testament | New Testament | Psalm |
|---|---|---|---|
| Day 163 | 1 Kings 8:1–53 | John 19:25b–42 | Psalm 92:1–9 |
| Day 164 | 1 Kings 8:54–10:13 | John 20:1–18 | Psalm 92:10–15 |
| Day 165 | 1 Kings 10:14–11:43 | John 20:19–31 | Psalm 93 |
| Day 166 | 1 Kings 12:1–13:10 | John 21 | Psalm 94:1–11 |
| Day 167 | 1 Kings 13:11–14:31 | Acts 1:1–11 | Psalm 94:12–23 |
| Day 168 | 1 Kings 15:1–16:20 | Acts 1:12–26 | Psalm 95 |
| Day 169 | 1 Kings 16:21–18:19 | Acts 2:1–21 | Psalm 96:1–8 |
| Day 170 | 1 Kings 18:20–19:21 | Acts 2:22–41 | Psalm 96:9–13 |
| Day 171 | 1 Kings 20 | Acts 2:42–3:26 | Psalm 97:1–6 |
| Day 172 | 1 Kings 21:1–22:28 | Acts 4:1–22 | Psalm 97:7–12 |
| Day 173 | 1 Kings 22:29–2 Kings 1:18 | Acts 4:23–5:11 | Psalm 98 |
| Day 174 | 2 Kings 2–3 | Acts 5:12–28 | Psalm 99 |
| Day 175 | 2 Kings 4 | Acts 5:29–6:15 | Psalm 100 |
| Day 176 | 2 Kings 5:1–6:23 | Acts 7:1–16 | Psalm 101 |
| Day 177 | 2 Kings 6:24–8:15 | Acts 7:17–36 | Psalm 102:1–7 |
| Day 178 | 2 Kings 8:16–9:37 | Acts 7:37–53 | Psalm 102:8–17 |
| Day 179 | 2 Kings 10–11 | Acts 7:54–8:8 | Psalm 102:18–28 |
| Day 180 | 2 Kings 12–13 | Acts 8:9–40 | Psalm 103:1–9 |
| Day 181 | 2 Kings 14–15 | Acts 9:1–16 | Psalm 103:10–14 |
| Day 182 | 2 Kings 16–17 | Acts 9:17–31 | Psalm 103:15–22 |
| Day 183 | 2 Kings 18:1–19:7 | Acts 9:32–10:16 | Psalm 104:1–9 |
| Day 184 | 2 Kings 19:8–20:21 | Acts 10:17–33 | Psalm 104:10–23 |
| Day 185 | 2 Kings 21–22 | Acts 10:34–11:18 | Psalm 104:24–30 |
| Day 186 | 2 Kings 23 | Acts 11:19–12:17 | Psalm 104:31–35 |
| Day 187 | 2 Kings 24–25 | Acts 12:18–13:13 | Psalm 105:1–7 |
| Day 188 | 1 Chronicles 1–2 | Acts 13:14–43 | Psalm 105:8–15 |
| Day 189 | 1 Chronicles 3:1–5:10 | Acts 13:44–14:10 | Psalm 105:16–28 |
| Day 190 | 1 Chronicles 5:11–6:81 | Acts 14:11–28 | Psalm 105:29–36 |
| Day 191 | 1 Chronicles 7:1–9:9 | Acts 15:1–18 | Psalm 105:37–45 |
| Day 192 | 1 Chronicles 9:10–11:9 | Acts 15:19–41 | Psalm 106:1–12 |
| Day 193 | 1 Chronicles 11:10–12:40 | Acts 16:1–15 | Psalm 106:13–27 |
| Day 194 | 1 Chronicles 13–15 | Acts 16:16–40 | Psalm 106:28–33 |
| Day 195 | 1 Chronicles 16–17 | Acts 17:1–14 | Psalm 106:34–43 |
| Day 196 | 1 Chronicles 18–20 | Acts 17:15–34 | Psalm 106:44–48 |
| Day 197 | 1 Chronicles 21–22 | Acts 18:1–23 | Psalm 107:1–9 |

# APPENDIX A

| | | | |
|---|---|---|---|
| Day 198 | 1 Chronicles 23–25 | Acts 19:1–10:10 | Psalm 107:10–16 |
| Day 199 | 1 Chronicles 26–27 | Acts 19:11–22 | Psalm 107:17–32 |
| Day 200 | 1 Chronicles 28–29 | Acts 19:23–41 | Psalm 107:33–38 |
| Day 201 | 2 Chronicles 1–3 | Acts 20:1–16 | Psalm 107:39–43 |
| Day 202 | 2 Chronicles 4:1–6:11 | Acts 20:17–38 | Psalm 108 |
| Day 203 | 2 Chronicles 6:12–7:10 | Acts 21:1–14 | Psalm 109:1–20 |
| Day 204 | 2 Chronicles 7:11–9:28 | Acts 21:15–32 | Psalm 109:21–31 |
| Day 205 | 2 Chronicles 9:29–12:16 | Acts 21:33–22:16 | Psalm 110:1–3 |
| Day 206 | 2 Chronicles 13–15 | Acts 22:17–23:11 | Psalm 110:4–7 |
| Day 207 | 2 Chronicles 16–17 | Acts 23:12–24:21 | Psalm 111 |
| Day 208 | 2 Chronicles 18–19 | Acts 24:22–25:12 | Psalm 112 |
| Day 209 | 2 Chronicles 20–21 | Acts 25:13–27 | Psalm 113 |
| Day 210 | 2 Chronicles 22–23 | Acts 26 | Psalm 114 |
| Day 211 | 2 Chronicles 24:1–25:16 | Acts 27:1–20 | Psalm 115:1–10 |
| Day 212 | 2 Chronicles 25:17–27:9 | Acts 27:21–28:6 | Psalm 115:11–18 |
| Day 213 | 2 Chronicles 28:1–29:19 | Acts 28:7–31 | Psalm 116:1–5 |
| Day 214 | 2 Chronicles 29:20–30:27 | Romans 1:1–17 | Psalm 116:6–19 |
| Day 215 | 2 Chronicles 31–32 | Romans 1:18–32 | Psalm 117 |
| Day 216 | 2 Chronicles 33:1–34:7 | Romans 2 | Psalm 118:1–18 |
| Day 217 | 2 Chronicles 34:8–35:19 | Romans 3:1–26 | Psalm 118:19–23 |
| Day 218 | 2 Chronicles 35:20–36:23 | Romans 3:27–4:25 | Psalm 118:24–29 |
| Day 219 | Ezra 1–3 | Romans 5 | Psalm 119:1–8 |
| Day 220 | Ezra 4–5 | Romans 6:1–7:6 | Psalm 119:9–16 |
| Day 221 | Ezra 6:1–7:26 | Romans 7:7–25 | Psalm 119:17–32 |
| Day 222 | Ezra 7:27–9:4 | Romans 8:1–27 | Psalm 119:33–40 |
| Day 223 | Ezra 9:5–10:44 | Romans 8:28–39 | Psalm 119:41–64 |
| Day 224 | Nehemiah 1:1–3:16 | Romans 9:1–18 | Psalm 119:65–72 |
| Day 225 | Nehemiah 3:17–5:13 | Romans 9:19–33 | Psalm 119:73–80 |
| Day 226 | Nehemiah 5:14–7:73 | Romans 10:1–13 | Psalm 119:81–88 |
| Day 227 | Nehemiah 8:1–9:5 | Romans 10:14–11:24 | Psalm 119:89–104 |
| Day 228 | Nehemiah 9:6–10:27 | Romans 11:25–12:8 | Psalm 119:105–120 |
| Day 229 | Nehemiah 10:28–12:26 | Romans 12:9–13:7 | Psalm 119:121–128 |
| Day 230 | Nehemiah 12:27–13:31 | Romans 13:8–14:12 | Psalm 119:129–136 |
| Day 231 | Esther 1:1–2:18 | Romans 14:13–15:13 | Psalm 119:137–152 |
| Day 232 | Esther 2:19–5:14 | Romans 15:14–21 | Psalm 119:153–168 |

| | | | |
|---|---|---|---|
| **Day 233** | Esther 6–8 | Romans 15:22–33 | Psalm 119:169–176 |
| **Day 234** | Esther 9–10 | Romans 16 | Psalms 120–122 |
| **Day 235** | Job 1–3 | 1 Corinthians 1:1–25 | Psalm 123 |
| **Day 236** | Job 4–6 | 1 Corinthians 1:26–2:16 | Psalms 124–125 |
| **Day 237** | Job 7–9 | 1 Corinthians 3 | Psalms 126–127 |
| **Day 238** | Job 10–13 | 1 Corinthians 4:1–13 | Psalms 128–129 |
| **Day 239** | Job 14–16 | 1 Corinthians 4:14–5:13 | Psalm 130 |
| **Day 240** | Job 17–20 | 1 Corinthians 6 | Psalm 131 |
| **Day 241** | Job 21–23 | 1 Corinthians 7:1–16 | Psalm 132 |
| **Day 242** | Job 24–27 | 1 Corinthians 7:17–40 | Psalms 133–134 |
| **Day 243** | Job 28–30 | 1 Corinthians 8 | Psalm 135 |
| **Day 244** | Job 31–33 | 1 Corinthians 9:1–18 | Psalm 136:1–9 |
| **Day 245** | Job 34–36 | 1 Corinthians 9:19–10:13 | Psalm 136:10–26 |
| **Day 246** | Job 37–39 | 1 Corinthians 10:14–11:1 | Psalm 137 |
| **Day 247** | Job 40–42 | 1 Corinthians 11:2–34 | Psalm 138 |
| **Day 248** | Ecclesiastes 1:1–3:15 | 1 Corinthians 12:1–26 | Psalm 139:1–6 |
| **Day 249** | Ecclesiastes 3:16–6:12 | 1 Corinthians 12:27–13:13 | Psalm 139:7–18 |
| **Day 250** | Ecclesiastes 7:1–9:12 | 1 Corinthians 14:1–22 | Psalm 139:19–24 |
| **Day 251** | Ecclesiastes 9:13–12:14 | 1 Corinthians 14:23–15:11 | Psalm 140:1–8 |
| **Day 252** | Song of Solomon 1–4 | 1 Corinthians 15:12–34 | Psalm 140:9–13 |
| **Day 253** | Song of Solomon 5–8 | 1 Corinthians 15:35–58 | Psalm 141 |
| **Day 254** | Isaiah 1–2 | 1 Corinthians 16 | Psalm 142 |
| **Day 255** | Isaiah 3–5 | 2 Corinthians 1:1–11 | Psalm 143:1–6 |
| **Day 256** | Isaiah 6–8 | 2 Corinthians 1:12–2:4 | Psalm 143:7–12 |
| **Day 257** | Isaiah 9–10 | 2 Corinthians 2:5–17 | Psalm 144 |
| **Day 258** | Isaiah 11–13 | 2 Corinthians 3 | Psalm 145 |
| **Day 259** | Isaiah 14–16 | 2 Corinthians 4 | Psalm 146 |
| **Day 260** | Isaiah 17–19 | 2 Corinthians 5 | Psalm 147:1–11 |
| **Day 261** | Isaiah 20–23 | 2 Corinthians 6 | Psalm 147:12–20 |
| **Day 262** | Isaiah 24:1–26:19 | 2 Corinthians 7 | Psalm 148 |
| **Day 263** | Isaiah 26:20–28:29 | 2 Corinthians 8 | Psalms 149–150 |
| **Day 264** | Isaiah 29–30 | 2 Corinthians 9 | Proverbs 1:1–9 |
| **Day 265** | Isaiah 31–33 | 2 Corinthians 10 | Proverbs 1:10–22 |
| **Day 266** | Isaiah 34–36 | 2 Corinthians 11 | Proverbs 1:23–26 |
| **Day 267** | Isaiah 37–38 | 2 Corinthians 12:1–10 | Proverbs 1:27–33 |

# APPENDIX A

|  | | | |
|---|---|---|---|
| Day 268 | Isaiah 39–40 | 2 Corinthians 10:11–13:14 | Proverbs 2:1–15 |
| Day 269 | Isaiah 41–42 | Galatians 1 | Proverbs 2:16–22 |
| Day 270 | Isaiah 43:1–44:20 | Galatians 2 | Proverbs 3:1–12 |
| Day 271 | Isaiah 44:21–46:13 | Galatians 3:1–18 | Proverbs 3:13–26 |
| Day 272 | Isaiah 47:1–49:13 | Galatians 3:19–29 | Proverbs 3:27–35 |
| Day 273 | Isaiah 49:14–51:23 | Galatians 4:1–11 | Proverbs 4:1–19 |
| Day 274 | Isaiah 52–54 | Galatians 4:12–31 | Proverbs 4:20–27 |
| Day 275 | Isaiah 55–57 | Galatians 5 | Proverbs 5:1–14 |
| Day 276 | Isaiah 58–59 | Galatians 6 | Proverbs 5:15–23 |
| Day 277 | Isaiah 60–62 | Ephesians 1 | Proverbs 6:1–5 |
| Day 278 | Isaiah 63:1–65:16 | Ephesians 2 | Proverbs 6:6–19 |
| Day 279 | Isaiah 65:17–66:24 | Ephesians 3:1–4:16 | Proverbs 6:20–26 |
| Day 280 | Jeremiah 1–2 | Ephesians 4:17–32 | Proverbs 6:27–35 |
| Day 281 | Jeremiah 3:1–4:22 | Ephesians 5 | Proverbs 7:1–5 |
| Day 282 | Jeremiah 4:23–5:31 | Ephesians 6 | Proverbs 7:6–27 |
| Day 283 | Jeremiah 6:1–7:26 | Philippians 1:1–26 | Proverbs 8:1–11 |
| Day 284 | Jeremiah 7:27–9:16 | Philippians 1:27–2:18 | Proverbs 8:12–21 |
| Day 285 | Jeremiah 9:17–11:17 | Philippians 2:19–30 | Proverbs 8:22–36 |
| Day 286 | Jeremiah 11:18–13:27 | Philippians 3 | Proverbs 9:1–6 |
| Day 287 | Jeremiah 14–15 | Philippians 4 | Proverbs 9:7–18 |
| Day 288 | Jeremiah 16–17 | Colossians 1:1–23 | Proverbs 10:1–5 |
| Day 289 | Jeremiah 18:1–20:6 | Colossians 1:24–2:15 | Proverbs 10:6–14 |
| Day 290 | Jeremiah 20:7–22:19 | Colossians 2:16–3:4 | Proverbs 10:15–26 |
| Day 291 | Jeremiah 22:20–23:40 | Colossians 3:5–4:1 | Proverbs 10:27–32 |
| Day 292 | Jeremiah 24–25 | Colossians 4:2–18 | Proverbs 11:1–11 |
| Day 293 | Jeremiah 26–27 | 1 Thessalonians 1:1–2:8 | Proverbs 11:12–21 |
| Day 294 | Jeremiah 28–29 | 1 Thessalonians 2:9–3:13 | Proverbs 11:22–26 |
| Day 295 | Jeremiah 30:1–31:22 | 1 Thessalonians 4:1–5:11 | Proverbs 11:27–31 |
| Day 296 | Jeremiah 31:23–32:35 | 1 Thessalonians 5:12–28 | Proverbs 12:1–14 |
| Day 297 | Jeremiah 32:36–34:7 | 2 Thessalonians 1–2 | Proverbs 12:15–20 |
| Day 298 | Jeremiah 34:8–36:10 | 2 Thessalonians 3 | Proverbs 12:21–28 |
| Day 299 | Jeremiah 36:11–38:13 | 1 Timothy 1:1–17 | Proverbs 13:1–4 |
| Day 300 | Jeremiah 38:14–40:6 | 1 Timothy 1:18–3:13 | Proverbs 13:5–13 |
| Day 301 | Jeremiah 40:7–42:22 | 1 Timothy 3:14–4:10 | Proverbs 13:14–21 |
| Day 302 | Jeremiah 43–44 | 1 Timothy 4:11–5:16 | Proverbs 13:22–25 |

| | | | |
|---|---|---|---|
| Day 303 | Jeremiah 45–47 | 1 Timothy 5:17–6:21 | Proverbs 14:1–6 |
| Day 304 | Jeremiah 48:1–49:6 | 2 Timothy 1 | Proverbs 14:7–22 |
| Day 305 | Jeremiah 49:7–50:16 | 2 Timothy 2 | Proverbs 14:23–27 |
| Day 306 | Jeremiah 50:17–51:14 | 2 Timothy 3 | Proverbs 14:28–35 |
| Day 307 | Jeremiah 51:15–64 | 2 Timothy 4 | Proverbs 15:1–9 |
| Day 308 | Jeremiah 52–Lamentations 1 | Titus 1:1–9 | Proverbs 15:10–17 |
| Day 309 | Lamentations 2:1–3:38 | Titus 1:10–2:15 | Proverbs 15:18–26 |
| Day 310 | Lamentations 3:39–5:22 | Titus 3 | Proverbs 15:27–33 |
| Day 311 | Ezekiel 1:1–3:21 | Philemon 1 | Proverbs 16:1–9 |
| Day 312 | Ezekiel 3:22–5:17 | Hebrews 1:1–2:4 | Proverbs 16:10–21 |
| Day 313 | Ezekiel 6–7 | Hebrews 2:5–18 | Proverbs 16:22–33 |
| Day 314 | Ezekiel 8–10 | Hebrews 3:1–4:3 | Proverbs 17:1–5 |
| Day 315 | Ezekiel 11–12 | Hebrews 4:4–5:10 | Proverbs 17:6–12 |
| Day 316 | Ezekiel 13–14 | Hebrews 5:11–6:20 | Proverbs 17:13–22 |
| Day 317 | Ezekiel 15:1–16:43 | Hebrews 7:1–28 | Proverbs 17:23–28 |
| Day 318 | Ezekiel 16:44–17:24 | Hebrews 8:1–9:10 | Proverbs 18:1–7 |
| Day 319 | Ezekiel 18–19 | Hebrews 9:11–28 | Proverbs 18:8–17 |
| Day 320 | Ezekiel 20 | Hebrews 10:1–25 | Proverbs 18:18–24 |
| Day 321 | Ezekiel 21–22 | Hebrews 10:26–39 | Proverbs 19:1–8 |
| Day 322 | Ezekiel 23 | Hebrews 11:1–31 | Proverbs 19:9–14 |
| Day 323 | Ezekiel 24–26 | Hebrews 11:32–40 | Proverbs 19:15–21 |
| Day 324 | Ezekiel 27–28 | Hebrews 12:1–13 | Proverbs 19:22–29 |
| Day 325 | Ezekiel 29–30 | Hebrews 12:14–29 | Proverbs 20:1–18 |
| Day 326 | Ezekiel 31–32 | Hebrews 13 | Proverbs 20:19–24 |
| Day 327 | Ezekiel 33:1–34:10 | James 1 | Proverbs 20:25–30 |
| Day 328 | Ezekiel 34:11–36:15 | James 2 | Proverbs 21:1–8 |
| Day 329 | Ezekiel 36:16–37:28 | James 3 | Proverbs 21:9–18 |
| Day 330 | Ezekiel 38–39 | James 4:1–5:6 | Proverbs 21:19–24 |
| Day 331 | Ezekiel 40 | James 5:7–20 | Proverbs 21:25–31 |
| Day 332 | Ezekiel 41:1–43:12 | 1 Peter 1:1–12 | Proverbs 22:1–9 |
| Day 333 | Ezekiel 43:13–44:31 | 1 Peter 1:13–2:3 | Proverbs 22:10–23 |
| Day 334 | Ezekiel 45–46 | 1 Peter 2:4–17 | Proverbs 22:24–29 |
| Day 335 | Ezekiel 47–48 | 1 Peter 2:18–3:7 | Proverbs 23:1–9 |
| Day 336 | Daniel 1:1–2:23 | 1 Peter 3:8–4:19 | Proverbs 23:10–16 |
| Day 337 | Daniel 2:24–3:30 | 1 Peter 5 | Proverbs 23:17–25 |

# APPENDIX A

| | | | |
|---|---|---|---|
| Day 338 | Daniel 4 | 2 Peter 1 | Proverbs 23:26–35 |
| Day 339 | Daniel 5 | 2 Peter 2 | Proverbs 24:1–18 |
| Day 340 | Daniel 6:1–7:14 | 2 Peter 3 | Proverbs 24:19–27 |
| Day 341 | Daniel 7:15–8:27 | 1 John 1:1–2:17 | Proverbs 24:28–34 |
| Day 342 | Daniel 9–10 | 1 John 2:18–29 | Proverbs 25:1–12 |
| Day 343 | Daniel 11–12 | 1 John 3:1–12 | Proverbs 25:13–17 |
| Day 344 | Hosea 1–3 | 1 John 3:13–4:16 | Proverbs 25:18–28 |
| Day 345 | Hosea 4–6 | 1 John 4:17–5:21 | Proverbs 26:1–16 |
| Day 346 | Hosea 7–10 | 2 John | Proverbs 26:17–21 |
| Day 347 | Hosea 11–14 | 3 John | Proverbs 26:22–27:9 |
| Day 348 | Joel 1:1–2:17 | Jude | Proverbs 27:10–17 |
| Day 349 | Joel 2:18–3:21 | Revelation 1:1–2:11 | Proverbs 27:18–27 |
| Day 350 | Amos 1:1–4:5 | Revelation 2:12–29 | Proverbs 28:1–8 |
| Day 351 | Amos 4:6–6:14 | Revelation 3 | Proverbs 28:9–16 |
| Day 352 | Amos 7–9 | Revelation 4:1–5:5 | Proverbs 28:17–24 |
| Day 353 | Obadiah and Jonah | Revelation 5:6–14 | Proverbs 28:25–28 |
| Day 354 | Micah 1:1–4:5 | Revelation 6:1–7:8 | Proverbs 29:1–8 |
| Day 355 | Micah 4:6–7:20 | Revelation 7:9–8:13 | Proverbs 29:9–14 |
| Day 356 | Nahum 1–3 | Revelation 9–10 | Proverbs 29:15–23 |
| Day 357 | Habakkuk 1–3 | Revelation 11 | Proverbs 29:24–27 |
| Day 358 | Zephaniah 1–3 | Revelation 12 | Proverbs 30:1–6 |
| Day 359 | Haggai 1–2 | Revelation 13:1–14:13 | Proverbs 30:7–16 |
| Day 360 | Zechariah 1–4 | Revelation 14:14–16:3 | Proverbs 30:17–20 |
| Day 361 | Zechariah 5–8 | Revelation 16:4–21 | Proverbs 30:21–28 |
| Day 362 | Zechariah 9–11 | Revelation 17:1–18:8 | Proverbs 30:29–33 |
| Day 363 | Zechariah 12–14 | Revelation 18:9–24 | Proverbs 31:1–9 |
| Day 364 | Malachi 1–2 | Revelation 19–20 | Proverbs 31:10–17 |
| Day 365 | Malachi 3–4 | Revelation 21–22 | Proverbs 31:18–31 |

# APPENDIX B

## Timeline of Important Biblical Events

About 4000 BC—The Fall
About 2350 BC—The Flood
About 2235 BC—Dispersion of the races
About 2100–1500 BC—Age of the Patriarchs
About 1950 BC—Amorites conquer Mesopotamia
About 1925 BC—Call of Abraham
About 1720 BC—Joseph becomes governor of Egypt
About 1635 BC—Joseph's death
About 1575 BC—Birth of Moses
About 1500–1200 BC—Exodus and Promised Land conquest
About 1492 BC—Exodus from Egypt
About 1452 BC—Joshua appointed leader of the people of Israel
About 1451 BC—Crossing of the Jordan
About 1451–44 BC—Conquest of Canaan
About 1394–1095 BC—Period of the Judges
About 1095–1055 BC—King Saul, Israel's first monarch
About 1055–1015 BC—King David
About 1050 BC—Philistines settle in southern Palestine
About 1015–975 BC—King Solomon
About 1005 BC—Dedication of the Temple
About 975–587—The divided kingdom (Judah and Israel)

# APPENDIX B

About 721 BC—Captivity of Israel
About 587 BC—Babylonian Captivity (Judah)
About 535 BC—Return of the Jews to Jerusalem under Zerubbabel
About 515 BC—Second Temple dedicated
About 458 BC—Ezra leads second wave of Jews back to Jerusalem
About 445 BC—Nehemiah returns to Jerusalem and begins rebuilding city walls
About 37 BC–AD 4—Reign of Herod the Great, Roman-appointed king of Judea
About 4 BC–AD 6—Rule of Herod Archelaus, ethnarch (governor) of Judea, Samaria, and Idumea
About 4 BC–AD 34—Rule of Herod Philip, tetrarch of Iturea and Trachonitis
About 4 BC–AD 39—Rule of Herod Antipas, tetrarch (governor) of Galilee and Perea
About 6-4 BC—Birth of Jesus Christ
About 2 BC—Birth of Saul of Tarsus (later known as the apostle Paul)
About AD 20—Reconstruction of the Temple begins
About AD 25–27—Jesus' baptism
About AD 25–28—Ministry of John the Baptist
About AD 26–37—Pontius Pilate, prefect (official who enforces the law) of Judea
About AD 29–30—Christ's crucifixion and resurrection
About AD 31–37—Conversion of Saul of Tarsus (the apostle Paul)
About AD 31–95—Books of the New Testament written
About AD 45–58—The apostle Paul's missionary journeys
About AD 59–60—Paul's first imprisonment begins
About AD 67–68—Paul's final imprisonment and death in Rome

# APPENDIX C

## Important Dates (and Facts) in Bible Writing, Translation, and Publishing

**About 1400 BC**— The Ten Commandments delivered to Moses

**About 500–400 BC**—Completion of Hebrew manuscripts that would become the 39 Old Testament books

**Third and second centuries BC**—Completion of the Septuagint, a translation of all 39 books of the Old Testament canon and the 14 books of the Apocrypha into Greek

**First century AD**—Completion of all original manuscripts that make up the 27 New Testament books

**About 315**—Athanasius, bishop of Alexandria, identifies the 27 books of the New Testament

**About 362**—Council of Laodicea adopts canon of Old and New Testaments and the Apocrypha

**393**—Council of Hippo affirms canon of New Testament

**397**—Council of Carthage affirms canon of New Testament

**About 400**—Jerome completes the Latin Vulgate, a Greek manuscript containing the 39 books of the Old Testament, the 27 books of the New Testament, and the 14 books of the Apocrypha

**995**—Anglo-Saxon (early roots of English language) translations of the New Testament

**About 1207–28**—Archbishop of Canterbury Cardinal Stephen Langdon believed to have divided Bible into chapters and verses still used today

**About 1246**—Cardinal Hugo de Sancto Caro introduces system of Bible chapters

**1384**—Death of John Wycliffe, who had started the translation of the Bible (the 66 books in the canon of scripture as well as the Apocrypha) into English. The work was completed after his death.

**About 1455**—German inventor Johannes Gutenberg develops movable-type printing press, allowing for mass production of books. The first book printed is the Gutenberg Bible.

**1516**—Dutch theologian Desiderius Erasmus produces Greek/Latin parallel New Testament

# APPENDIX C

1522—Martin Luther's German New Testament published

1526—William Tyndale's complete New Testament, the first printed in English

1534—Martin Luther's complete German translation published

1535—Myles Coverdale's Bible, the first complete Bible in English, printed

1537—Matthew-Tyndale Bible, the second complete Bible printed in English. Done by John "Thomas Matthew" Rogers

1539—The Great Bible, the first English-language Bible authorized for public use, printed

1560—The Geneva Bible, the first English-language Bible to include chapter and verse references, printed

1568—The Bishops' Bible printed; revised substantially in 1572; the revised edition was the base text for the King James Version of 1611

1609—The Douay Old Testament and the Rheims New Testament (produced in 1582) are combined to make the first complete English Catholic Bible

1611—The King James Bible, including the Apocrypha, printed; Apocrypha removed in 1885, leaving the 66 books we have today

1782—Robert Aitken's Bible (King James Version), the first English-language Bible printed in America, published

1885—The English Revised Version Bible, the first major revision of the King James Version, published

1900—American publishing company Thomas Nelson & Sons publishes the American Standard Version Old Testament; the following year, the company released the entire Bible, the first major American revision of the King James Bible

1952—The Revised Standard Version published

1965—The Amplified Bible published

1971—The New American Standard Bible and *The Living Bible* published

1978—The complete New International Version (NIV) published

1982—The complete New King James Version published

1996—The complete New Living Translation published

2002—The complete Bible paraphrase, *The Message*, published

2004—Holman Christian Standard Bible published

# ART CREDITS

**Clipart.com:** Page 27, 44, 45, 94, 98, 107, 109, 114, 116, 121

**iStockphoto.com:** Page 19, 21, 111

**Shutterstock:** Cover, Page 7, 9, 10, 12–14, 16, 19, 20, 23–27, 29, 30, 33, 35, 37–42, 44, 46, 48, 49, 51, 53–58, 60–62, 64, 65, 67, 69, 73, 75–85, 87, 89, 91, 93, 94, 96, 97, 99, 100, 102–107, 109, 112–116, 118–120, 122–125, 127–139, 141, 143, 145, 150, 158

**Wikimedia:** Page 21, 30–35, 38, 42, 43, 47, 50, 52, 54, 57, 59, 63, 65, 66, 69, 70–72, 74, 75, 79, 80, 86, 90, 92, 95, 97, 111, 117, 119, 124, 128, 129, 142, 144